"Here is a book that offers both a thoroughly clear exposition of the writers who've been called the first Christian philosophers, and a guide to how their thoughts might relate to the challenge of making good intellectual sense of Christianity today. It is a learned, accessible, insightful survey of one of the great formative periods in the history of the Christian mind."

—Rowan Williams, University of Cambridge

"This thoughtful and scholarly book has revived my appreciation of the Apologists and my desire to re-read them. It provides an accessible introduction for those who have not encountered them before and a fresh and insightful reading for those who know them well. For both it invites reflection on some of the important issues they still raise for us today."

—Carol Harrison, University of Oxford

"Alvyn Pettersen presents his considerable scholarship in an accessible and engaging manner. In this very helpful study of the letters of six second-century Apologists and their refutation of charges against Christians of being atheists, cannibals, and partakers in incest, he gives us not only fascinating historical insights but food for thought concerning the business of apologetics in our own age and, indeed, the very nature of the Christian faith."

—John Inge, Bishop of Worcester, UK

THE SECOND-CENTURY APOLOGISTS

CASCADE COMPANIONS

The Christian theological tradition provides an embarrassment of riches: from Scripture to modern scholarship, we are blessed with a vast and complex theological inheritance. And yet this feast of traditional riches is too frequently inaccessible to the general reader.

The Cascade Companions series addresses the challenge by publishing books that combine academic rigor with broad appeal and readability. They aim to introduce nonspecialist readers to that vital storehouse of authors, documents, themes, histories, arguments, and movements that comprise this heritage with brief yet compelling volumes.

RECENT TITLES IN THIS SERIES:

THE SECOND-
CENTURY
APOLOGISTS

ALVYN PETTERSEN

CASCADE *Books* • Eugene, Oregon

THE SECOND-CENTURY APOLOGISTS

Cascade Companions

Cascade Books
An Imprint of Wipf and Stock Publishers
199 W. 8th Ave., Suite 3
Eugene, OR 97401

www.wipfandstock.com

PAPERBACK ISBN: 978-1-7252-6535-6
HARDCOVER ISBN: 978-1-7252-6526-4
EBOOK ISBN: 978-1-7252-6527-1

Cataloguing-in-Publication data:

Names: Pettersen, Alvyn, author.

Title: The second-century apologists / by Alvyn Pettersen.

Description: Eugene, OR: Cascade Books, 2020 | Series: Cas-
cade Companions | Includes bibliographical references and
index.

Identifiers: ISBN 978-1-7252-6535-6 (paperback) | ISBN 978-1-
7252-6526-4 (hardcover) | ISBN 978-1-7252-6527-1 (ebook)

Subjects: LCSH: Apologetics—History—Early church, ca. 30–
600 | Aristides—active 2nd century—Apology for the Christian
faith | Epistle to Diognetus | Justin—Martyr Saint | Tatian, ca.
120–173 | Athenagoras—active 2nd century | Theophilos—
Saint—active 2nd century | Christianity—Philosophy—History

Classification: BT1115 P48 2020 (print) | BT1115 (ebook)

Manufactured in the U.S.A.   08/28/20

To Catherine, Robert, and Elizabeth,
two daughters and a son in whom I
delight and of whom I am very proud

CONTENTS

ACKNOWLEDGMENTS

MY THANKS ARE DUE to many. In particular, I wish to thank the Chapter of Worcester Cathedral for granting me a sabbatical during which I began the research that underlies the content of this book. I am immensely grateful to the Rector and Fellows of Exeter College, Oxford, for electing me to a visiting Fellowship for the period of my sabbatical. This offered me very generous and convivial hospitality. Above all, it greatly facilitated my research, and provided rich intellectual stimulus both within and beyond the College. I am very appreciative of the wise, supportive, but not uncritical friendship which both Professor Carol Harrison, of Christ Church, Oxford, and Dr Rowan Williams, Master of Magdalene College, Cambridge, have extended to me, especially as I have been writing this book. Above all, I wish to thank my family. They have been patient and encouraging, ever urging me to return to my study in the basement, or, as they termed it, the dungeon of our house. "Back to the dungeon, dungeon troll," they would say. "The book calls." To each and all I am most thankful.

Alvyn Pettersen

Oxford, March 2020

INTRODUCTION

THIS BOOK LOOKS AT the writings of six Christian Apologists of the mid-to-late second century as they responded to some of the charges levelled against their Christian contemporaries. Then the faith of Christians was accused of being novel and, since truth was then generally associated with antiquity, of being merely a recent human invention. Meanwhile Christians themselves were then charged with being atheists, cannibals, and partakers in incest,[1] charges based upon misunderstandings of Christian practices. The charge of atheism arose from the refusal by Christians to acknowledge the deities of the Greco-Roman world and to share in its cults. That of cannibalism originated in people's wrongly thinking that they had found in what little they knew of Christians celebrating the eucharist, with its dominical invitation to eat of the body and drink of the blood of Christ, echoes of the feast in which, according to the myths, Thyestes, entertained by his brother Atreus,

1. Athenagoras, *Plea*, 1.3.

unknowingly ate of the flesh of one of his own sons. The third charge was based in the wider public's misinterpreting the Christians both obeying the dominical injunction to "love one another" and sharing, in the course of the rite of the eucharist, the kiss of peace as evidence of the occurrence in real life of the mythical account of Oedipus's sexual intercourse with his mother Jocasta.

These several charges had been made against Christians over many years. Dio Cassius, writing about the Domitian persecutions of AD 96, recorded that "Domitian slew, amongst many others, Flavius Clemens . . . and Flavia Domitilla, against both [of whom] was brought a charge of atheism."[2] Pliny the Younger, writing in AD 112 to the emperor Trajan, reported that those who had been accused of being Christians and who then had denied their being Christians confirmed their denials by reciting a prayer to the gods of the empire, by making supplications, accompanied by offerings of incense and wine, to the emperor Trajan's statue, and by cursing Christ, each and all incontrovertible proof that they had abandoned their monotheistic faith.[3] These various practices, once enacted, proved to Greco-Roman minds that a person was not an atheist. For though they denied the Christ, they yet affirmed their readiness both to venerate the gods of the empire and to honor the imperial cult. Meanwhile, by not enacting such practices, which "those who really are Christians [could] not be made to do,"[4] people proved that they were indeed

2. Dio Cassius, *Epitome*, 67.14. This literary evidence does not, however, prove that Flavius Clemens was a Christian, and, although Christian tradition counted Flavia Domitilla a Christian, the evidence for her being so is not clear. What is clear is that, from c.150 onwards, Christians built a cemetery on land that once had belonged to Flavia Domitilla.

3. Pliny, *Letters*, 10.96. See also *Letters*, 10.97.

4. Pliny, *Letters*, 10.96.

atheists, people who would not acknowledge the gods of the imperial cult. In the same letter, Pliny further reported to Trajan that Christians bound themselves with an oath not to commit, *inter alia*, adultery,[5] a particular wrong perhaps mentioned as something to which members of the public believed that Christians were prone. Yet further, again in the self-same letter, Pliny recorded that Christians met in the evening "to take food", "ordinary and harmless food" Pliny added,[6] as though wishing to assure Trajan that Christians did not engage in cannibalistic customs. In Smyrna in 156 the crowds that called on the governor to slaughter some Christians who had been arrested, cried out, "away with these atheists";[7] and the same governor, trying to persuade the arrested Bishop Polycarp to recant his Christian faith, said to Polycarp, "swear by the genius of the emperor, . . . Say, away with the atheists [*sc.* Christians]."[8] Some four to five years later, but this time in Rome, a Christian of the name of Lucius questioned why a certain Urbicus had punished another Christian of the name of Ptolemy, and asked, "why have you punished this man, not as an adulterer, nor fornicator, . . . but simply as one who has only confessed that he is called by the name of Christian?"[9] Other crimes, those of murder and theft, were also mentioned by the questioning Lucius. The mention, however, of adultery, indeed, the mention of adultery as the first in the list of possible misdemeanors, may again not be unrelated to the common charge of incest frequently levelled against Christians. Yet another five years later, again in Rome, Justin and his companions were brought

5. Pliny, *Letters*, 10.96.7.

6. Pliny, *Letters*, 10.96.7.

7. *The Martyrdom of Polycarp*, 3.2.

8. *The Martyrdom of Polycarp*, 9.2.

9. Justin, *Apology*, 2.2.

before Rusticus, the prefect of Rome. To Rusticus's demand that they should "sacrifice to the imperial gods," Justin and those arrested with him asserted that they would offer no sacrifices to "idols."[10] The replacement here of Rusticus's imperial "gods" with Justin's "idols" tallies with such thinking as that which lies behind Justin's earlier statement that non-Christians "called [*sc.* evil demons] gods,"[11] which "gods" the Christians denied and because of which the Christians were called "atheists," a title that Justin confessed that Christians accepted "so far as gods of this sort [were] concerned, but not with respect to the most true God."[12] In Lyons in 177 there was further anti-Christian activity. There an arrested Christian of the name of Vettius Epagathus unsuccessfully sought to be granted a public hearing where he might put the case that Christians were innocent of the charges of atheism and impiety.[13] Another arrested Christian, Attalus, burning as he was fastening to the brazen seat of the amphitheater's pyre, in effect, roasted as a piece of meat on the grill of a barbecue, cried out to the watching crowds, "Look. What you are doing [*sc.* to me] is cannibalism. We Christians are not cannibals, nor do we perform any other sinful act."[14] Also arrested were some non-Christians servants of certain Christian households. Terrified lest they themselves might be subjected to the very torture that they saw their Christian owners suffering, and acting at the instigation of some soldiers, they "falsely accused the Christians of Oedipean marriages and of being those who dined in the manner of Thyestes."[15]

10. *Martyrdom of Justin and His Companions*, 4.

11. Justin, *Apology*, 1.5.

12. Justin, *Apology*, 1.6.

13. *The Letter of the Churches of Lyons and Vienne*, 9.

14. *The Letter of the Churches of Lyons and Vienne*, 52.

15. *The Letter of the Churches of Lyons and Vienne*, 14.

It would therefore seem that the charges, both of atheism and of being partakers in Thyestean feasts and Oedipean intercourse, were levelled—in the former case, explicitly, and in the latter two cases, at least implicitly— against Christians over much of the second century who lived as far afield as in the provinces of Asia and of Bithynia, and of Pontus in the East, in Rome, and in the province of Gaul in the West. Of these charges that of atheism seems to be the most frequently mentioned. This may be because the references to this charge, the penalty for which was death, appear mainly in Christian literature, for whose readers, to use the later language of Tertullian, the blood of the martyrs was the seed of the church.[16] It may also be because, in comparison with any punishment inflicted by the empire on those found guilty of acts of cannibalism and adultery, the penalty imposed on those found guilty of denying the gods of the imperial cults was savage and irrevocable. All the charges falsely levelled against Christians, if not fairly and properly addressed, led, Christians noted, to miscarriages of justice. However, of all these charges, the charge of atheism, when not fairly and properly addressed, led to an irreversible miscarriage of injustice. It, of all the charges, therefore especially cried out for an apology.

That said, it is yet understandable why the second-century Apologists did attend to the, in some sense, less serious charges of cannibalism and incest. Not to state that Christians did not engage in cannibalism would have allowed people to think that the violent killing of another person—of which not just cannibalism but also the exposure of unwanted infants and the trading in humans for gladiatorial shows were examples—was of little or no concern; and not to maintain that Christians did not participate in incest would have permitted people to believe that vows of

16. Tertullian, *Apology*, 50.

fidelity, in this particular case those between family members, and, by extension, those between a married couple and the one God who had instituted the honorable estate of marriage, were but matters of indifference. Indeed, the issue of indifference was then an important issue. For Christians then were being challenged to define and justify their commitment to the contingent world of time and matter, a challenge that, in relation to such matters as cannibalism and incest, called for a clear understanding of how to behave daily, in a godly way, in relation to one's neighbor and relative. That challenge, indeed, came from not only wider society but also certain gnostic Christians who were not without teachers who "taught that to taste meat offered to idols and to renounce without reservation the [Christian] faith in times of persecution were matters of indifference."[17] It therefore followed that for the Apologists not to defend Christians against the charges of being cannibals and of participating in incest potentially would not only have allowed for the misrepresenting what was, in fact, the case when it came to Christian behavior, but also have given ground to those who would have been morally lax in their treatment of fellow creatures and casual in their relationship with the Creator of all. What then seems to have been, in the eyes of some gnostic Christians, matters of indifference were, in the eyes of the mid-to-late second-century Apologists, anything but such. A robust apology therefore was not an option; it was *demanded*, even as a robust definition and justification of a proper and godly commitment to the contingent world of time and matter were.

More often than not the thinking of these second-century Apologists has been examined in terms of tracing the gradual development—or, for some, the evolution—over

17. So Basilides, fl. 140, taught. See Eusebius, *Ecclesiastical History* 4.7.7.

the early centuries of the doctrine of God. So, for example, J. N. D. Kelly treated the Apologists's thinking regarding "the Word" and "the Trinity" under the general title of The divine triad;[18] and A. Grillmeier explored the Logos doctrine of the Apologists in his book, *Christ in Christian Tradition*,[19] in a section entitled "The Foundation of Christology as Speculative Theology and the Emergence of Hellenism." More recently, Helen Rhee, in her book *Early Christian Literature: Christ and Culture in the Second and Third Centuries*,[20] has examined the many literary forms that early Christians used to confirm their self-identity within a wider and, at times, hostile Greco-Roman society. In comparison with the works of such scholars as Kelly, Grillmeier, and Rhee, this book concentrates on exploring the early Apologists's various responses to the charges often brought against the mid-to-late second-century Christians. It examines the theological and moral themes that inhabit the arguments of the several Apologies. It assumes that any absence of uniformity in the arguments of the Apologists is consequential upon both the *different contexts* in which the several Apologists found themselves and the *variety of the arguments* that they felt appropriate to advance. So, this book notes, for example, that the *Letter to Diognetus* was written less as a defense of Christianity and more as a response to questions raised by Diognetus regarding the Christian faith. It recognizes that Tatian, a convert from a mystery cult to Christianity, writing with all the vehemence of a convert, highlighted the errors of the world that he had forsaken. It acknowledges that a person like Athenagoras found himself writing in a quasi-forensic manner. Having

18. Kelly, *Early Christian Doctrine*, 95.

19. Grillmeier, *Christ in Christian Tradition*, 106.

20. Rhee focuses on Apologies, Apocryphal Acts, and Martyr Acts.

named three specific charges brought against Christians, namely, those of atheism, cannibalism, and incest, Athenagoras then proceeded to "meet each charge separately."[21] Alongside such variety this book points out that there is also a variety of ways in which the several Apologists then sought to persuade their different audiences. Theophilos, for example, to suit the Hellenistic and Jewish roots of his reader, the bookish Autolycus, drew his defense almost exclusively from texts from the Decalogue and the Gospel according to Matthew. Justin, in dialogue with the Jew Trypho, relied heavily on the Hebrew Scriptures. Yet, when Justin engaged with the wider audience of mid-to-late second-century Rome, for whom texts from the Hebrew Scriptures were not authoritative, he drew the attention of his readers both to descriptions of how Christians lived righteously and to examples of how the moral codes of different Hellenistic cities were inconsistent, and so mutually undermining. Athenagoras, meanwhile, drew widely on the resources of Hellenistic poets and philosophers to expose the errors of his critics and to highlight the truth of Christian beliefs and the innocence of a Christian lifestyle.

Given this variegation between the several writers, their contexts, audiences, and arguments, this book then further assumes that making comparisons between this and that Apologist and building a sense of theological development or evolution in thought from one Apologist to another is hazardous.

This book further aims to draw the reader's attention to any missional aspects in the writings of the different Apologists. It is argued that, in addition to (i) mounting defenses against what the Apologists saw as false charges and to (ii) maintaining that Christians were a help, and not a hindrance, to establishing and preserving the empire's

21. Athenagoras, *Plea*, 3.1—4.1.

peace and well-being, the Apologists were also concerned that (iii) their writings might be instruments by which those who as yet did not trust fully and wholly in the One whom they believed to be the only, true God might be brought to such a trust. So, descriptions of the Christian lifestyle were penned, not just to allow the readers to conclude that Christians were innocent of charges of immorality but also to allow reflective non-Christians to turn from all ungodly practices and to turn to walking in the ways of the one and only holy God. For some of these Apologists, such was their urgent sense of the need to prompt the conversion of Christianity's critics that they did not flinch from warning of the dire and eternal punishment to be meted out in the End-time to those who were still inimical towards both God and God's creatures. Indeed, not to issue such warnings was considered "beyond the pale." In short, the concern of a number of these mid-to-late second-century Apologists was the well-being of not only Christians falsely accused but also those who falsely accused Christians.

1

THE SECOND-CENTURY GRECO-ROMAN WORLD

THE SECOND-CENTURY GRECO-ROMAN WORLD, generally speaking, was one of confidence, peace, and prosperity. "Wars," Aelius Aristides of Smyrna wrote in c.145, "have so vanished as to be but legends of the past."[1] "A person travels," he continued, "from one country to another as though it were his homeland."[2] These reflections may, of course, be not wholly true. For they may well contain an element of flattery, having, at least nominally, been addressed to the emperor Antoninus Pius. Yet they are neither unparalleled nor out of keeping with what was generally acknowledged to be the case then.

1. Aelius Aristides, *Panegyric to Rome*, 26. 70.
2. Aelius Aristides, *Panegyric to Rome*, 26.100.

PEACE AND PROSPERITY IN THE EMPIRE

Certainly the early second-century empire was sufficiently confident and at ease with itself that it was able to tolerate irritating minorities such as Stoic philosophers and Christians. The emperor Trajan [98–117], commenting, for example, on the anonymous denunciations of Christians by inhabitants of the province of Pontus, maintained that such denunciations were "not in keeping with the spirit of the age."[3] Nor had the situation changed that much by the 170s when, in his *Plea*, the Christian Apologist Athenagoras wrote of the emperors Marcus Aurelius's and Commodus's humanity shown to all, of the equality of everyone before the law, and, assuming that it is more than a mere rhetorical flourish, of "the profound peace that prevailed in the empire."[4] Irenaeus, bishop of Lyons and Vienne [fl.178], meanwhile, wrote of the peace and security then enjoyed even by Christians. In words that echoed Aristides's, Irenaeus paid tribute to the imperial law, noting that through Rome's agency "the world [was] at peace and [even Christians could] walk the highways without fear and sail where [they] wished."[5]

Such self-confidence, peace, and security were due in large part to the above-average ability as soldiers and administrators of the rulers of the empire from Nerva [96–98] to Marcus Aurelius [161–180]. This ability these rulers put at the service of their overarching aims, made known to all through the coinage then circulating, namely *security*, with an ensuing freedom of movement, *growth in trade*, with an increasing prosperity for many, and a uniform system of *justice for all*; and these overarching imperial aims were then to

3. Pliny, *Letters*, 10.97.

4. Athenagoras, *Plea*, 1.2.

5. Irenaeus, *Against the Heresies*, 4.30.3.

be realized locally by a provincial élite. At the same time, the way in which the empire was understood was changing. The former *division* of "Greek" and "barbarian" was gradually giving way to the *distinction* between "Roman" and "non-Roman"; provinces increasingly were thought of as a part of the empire; and provincial élites were viewed as the equals of the élites in Italy, and even of those in Rome.

Peace and prosperity, it is true, were not unbroken. There were occasional raids by groups based in northern Africa and in parts of Asia Minor. There were, for example, intermittent persecutions of Christians in eastern Bithynia in 112 and in Gaul in 177. There was a resumption of the war against the Germans in 178. However, these were interruptions in an otherwise lengthy period of general political stability.

In this generally long season of peace, and as a result of it, almost every level of society of the many city-states of the second-century Greco-Roman world benefitted. Romanization led to better buildings being erected; streets increasingly were paved; public sanitation was greatly improved. It was, however, not only life in the individual city-states that was enhanced. So too were the relationships between the various city-states. For trade, common currency, and increasingly similar administrative systems began to bind not only individual city-state to individual city-state but also many city-states together within the one empire. No wonder then that Celsus, taunting Christians in c.178, wrote that whatever Christians received in this world, they received from the emperor.[6] Nor was Celsus alone in thinking so. By the end of the second century there were not many provincials who would have questioned the statement that the benefits that they all enjoyed derived from their emperor. Indeed, there were not many provincials who would have

6. See Origen, *Against Celsus*, 8.67.

balked at the suggestion that, in some sense, the emperor embodied the empire, even as the head of a family embodied a family. For, even as in a family, the traditional basis of Roman society, the *paterfamilias* exercised almost complete authority, especially in and through his providing for and protecting his family members, so any emperor, committed to following Augustus's example in rebuilding the empire's security and stability, exercised similar authority. In some sense, the emperor was the *paterfamilias* of the empire. He was the empire's ultimate provider and peace-maker. He was to be honored and obeyed.

That said, it is not possible to understand the second-century Greco-Roman Empire simply in terms of ruling emperors, well-administered provinces, and any ensuing peace and prosperity. For the empire then was not deemed to be secular in the modern sense of the word "secular." Celsus's thought that whatever people received in this world they had received from the emperor was held to be true by many. It was, however, also held by many to be less than the whole truth. For it was then also believed to be true that the *gods* of the Greco-Roman cults played a significant role in the maintenance of the empire's peace and prosperity. Without the *pax deorum*, the "peace of the gods" of the empire, there could be no *pax Romana*, Roman peace. Religion was therefore an inalienable part of daily life, in both the home and the public sphere.

RELIGION IN THE EMPIRE

The worship of the gods of the imperial cult was an ancient practice, founded upon the belief not only that the cult had helped individuals and their cities come into being, and then come so far and for so long, but also that, had the cult not been faithfully practiced, the life of the few for whom life had been bleak would have been yet bleaker. It was therefore commonly held that a person, and, by extension, a city, could not be too careful. It was better to honor all the gods than to offend even one. For even one offended god might wreak havoc on the life of a person or a community. It is true that some with philosophical inclinations had more sophisticated understandings of the gods. For instance, the Skeptics thought that the gods were modelled on people's social relationships on earth, that the cults and the images of the gods were valid only because they already existed, and that their purpose was but to promote civic cohesion. Platonists too approached the gods differently from the general populace, having long held that the Homeric epics and the ancient myths of the gods were allegories, that, when interpreted aright, explained the world and humanity's place within it. Such ideas, however, were too subtle for most people and were largely ineffective when it came to changing the attitudes and practices of the vast majority. So, the vast majority of people continued to worship the gods and practice the ancient cult. Indeed, an individual might continue to worship a number of gods, not necessarily in succession, but at one and the same time. Certainly, it must be admitted, an individual might adhere to one particular deity as his or her particular protector; but that individual would not have "converted" to that deity, to the exclusion of all other deities. Indeed, there was no need to "convert." For some understood a local god as the local expression of a god worshipped elsewhere and many operated with a form of polytheism, which, stripped to its essentials, could be reduced to the formula, "you cannot be too careful; so worship them all." An extreme example of this urge in late classical piety to cover all eventualities is manifest in the erection of an altar on the Areopagus in Athens dedicated to the "unknown god."[7] Furthermore, many, while honoring one

7. See Acts 17:23, which tells of the apostle Paul noticing such an

god, deemed to be the "high" god, were yet conscious that, in honoring their "high" god, they were, at one and the same time, also honoring lesser deities, subordinates of "their" one high god. For some, in fact, the more local, lesser deities were included in the Roman imperial pantheon, and the more these were honored, the fuller and the richer became the honor and worship of the one who was the "high" god of that pantheon. The worship of such a "high" god did not therefore amount to monotheism, even as it did not preclude a priest being a priest of more than one deity.

Such was possible for the vast majority of the second-century Greco-Roman world for two main reasons. Firstly, in the pursuit of religion it was *rites* that were important. What therefore the cult demanded of an individual was an *act*, particularly the religious ceremony of sacrificing to the gods. Secondly, there was no particular interest in a person's *beliefs*, no demand that an individual should affirm certain beliefs and deny others. So, to accuse people of being "atheists" was therefore to accuse them, not of failing to *believe* in a god or gods, but of being unwilling to engage in the *act* of sacrificing to the empire's gods, which, to most people then, amounted to both an unreadiness to honor the god or gods and a refusal to seek to appease them, and so to take part in the common effort to sustain or to restore the *pax Romana*. Heresy (*haeresis*) then, therefore, had no sense of "heresy" as now generally understood. Rather, it meant "choice," an individual's choosing the thinking and associated practices of one or more schools of thought. Thus, "heresy" for most people then bore not a sense of false doctrine but of choice, where no choice in and of itself was wrong. The opposite of heterodoxy therefore was not orthodoxy, but homodoxy, "agreement."

---

inscribed altar.

At least two social consequences followed from this. Firstly, given that, in the second-century empire, there was a galaxy of gods, a variety of cults, and a readiness of people to respect, if not to engage in, the differing religious practices of the time, *imperial religion*, not surprisingly, became a very strong, widely shared bond that held the empire together, particularly in times of internal turmoil and external threat.

Secondly, beliefs were important for people like the Jews and the Christians, even to the point of being the basis both used for excluding certain religious choices, certain "haereses," and for directing the doing of (or refraining from) particular acts, whatever the cost. Any belief-based resistance on the part of a Jew or a Christian to, for example, sacrificing to a Roman deity therefore reeked of obstinacy and intransigence.[8] Indeed, often it was interpreted as a standing in the way of that which united the empire, especially when the empire was particularly vulnerable to fragmentation. Such religious people seemed therefore to stand in marked contrast with those who practiced the cult of the empire; and their understandings of proper social engagement differed greatly.

Nor could these contrasts and differences be seen as easy bedfellows. Practicing the imperial cult involved the giving of gifts and the making of sacrifices, given and made in thanksgiving and for propitiation. As in daily life, so in the imperial cult, two themes dominated, that of personal honor and that of giving in order that one might receive in return. It was, therefore, thought, firstly, that deities, being not just important patrons but also powers of immense superiority, demanded the highest honors. Secondly, it was further believed that, if deities were not granted the highest honors, they might become angry. Thirdly, it was

8. Pliny, *Letters*, 10.96.

also thought that, although deities could be very generous givers, they were not *committed* givers, bound to giving regular gifts in return. For these reasons it was therefore necessary always to honor all gods (other people's as well as one's own), not to allow anyone to dishonor any gods through, for example, excluding themselves from the cults, and always to appease the gods, for fear lest they might, just possibly, be angry. For a person never knew if, when, or how a god might have been outraged; and if a god, by chance, had been outraged, that same person never knew whether the result would be that the god would then not support or would even punish that individual, his family or her city-state or empire. Such contrasted greatly with Christian beliefs, which insisted on monotheism, resisted the thought that people, mere creatures, could lay any claim upon God, the Creator of all, and maintained that God was ever faithful, always generous. God, Christians held, was to be honored, and the divine name was to be hallowed, simply and solely because God was God.

That people held that the gods of the empire needed appeasing is evidenced variously. A local leader might call upon his people to sacrifice to the local deities when he wished to win the favor of the gods in order to counter a local threat. A school teacher, introducing pupils to the Homeric myths, could not avoid those passages that spoke of gods being angered either by the absence or the dishonorable practice of sacrifice. Pausanias [c.110–180], given to rationalizing the more bizarre aspects of myths, nevertheless left untouched those that told of a god's anger, to be discerned in earthquakes and famines and to be appeased by people performing appropriate religious rituals at local shrines. In a speech to the Roman Senate in c.203, Manilius Fuscus, a future governor of Asia, advocated all due worship and veneration of the immortal gods, so as to ensure the continuing security of the empire. Marcus Aurelius [121–180] may have dismissed as superstition belief in the anger of the gods, but many of his contemporaries did not. Faced with famine or threat, they still consulted oracles, heeded the god's advice as to which rite would appease the divine wrath, and performed those commended, in order to persuade the heavens to end whatever evil had befallen them.

Alongside this worship of the gods there was also the cult of the emperor. For like the gods of the cult, emperors also were held to be powerful but unreliable benefactors, whom their subjects needed always to honor. In this "human" field the precept, "give to the giver that hopefully the giver may reciprocate, and not to the person who cannot reciprocate," was also to be followed. The powerful always needed to be gratified.

Very clearly the cult was an aspect of every part of a person's life. It was not simply a "leisure time" pursuit, the modern day equivalent of a "weekend" hobby. People of the second century "did god" in the temple and in civic life. They "did god" in education, in tradesmen's guilds, and in clubs. Their painters, engravers, and carvers could scarcely survive without making images of the gods or creating designs containing cultic symbols. Their soldiers had to swear loyalty to the "divine" emperor as well as to the god Mithras. Their emperor needed ever to be "kept sweet." In short, the cult was integral to daily life, and every citizen probably had a role in it. Further, people "did god" more indirectly. For the cult impacted upon local economies. At the most basic level, any meat bought in a market probably had been slaughtered as a sacrifice in a temple. The annual feasts of societies of tradesmen generally were held in the temple of their tutelary god, their meal previously having been offered to the gods. A cult often had its own funds, its gods receiving rents from lands, offerings from collection boxes, and taxes from sacrifices. Cults and their priest-hoods were therefore financially valuable. Not surprisingly therefore Greek cities increasingly both multiplied their priesthoods and then put these up for sale. In first-century Miletus, for example, the authorities decreed the number of sacrifices to be offered annually to the god Asclepius and stipulated that the cult priests should receive the hides, the entrails, and the best cuts of all animals sacrificed. This financially attractive lot the city authorities then sold, to the benefit of three parties: (i) the city authorities who devised and then auctioned the lot would have gained financially; (ii) whoever was successful in bidding for the cult's priest-hood benefitted from the cult's increased annual business; and (iii) local merchants and businesses found their services the more in demand, especially at the times of major festivals, when pilgrims required the services of not only the cult but also market traders and providers of accommodation. Anyone then who might oppose such a local cult could find themselves having to defend their position before, at the very least, the local cult, local businesses, and other interested parties. Witness the events in Ephesus where Demetrius, a silversmith who made silver shrines of Artemis, joined with others of the same trade, and rose up against the apostle Paul.[9]

CHRISTIANITY IN THE EMPIRE

Within this world Christianity was viewed with caution, if not suspicion. In comparison with the imperial cults and with Judaism it was seen as new. Its profession and practice were as yet unauthorized. Its followers met, not publicly, but privately, in house groups. Its teaching was open to anyone who would be a catechumen, but attendance at the

9. Acts 19:23–27.

eucharistic mysteries was permitted only to the baptized. For many, the imperial authorities included, Christianity was therefore a religion about which they could discover little. There were rumors of "love feasts," at which attendees were urged to love their brothers and sisters, greeting one another with a kiss. There was mention of gatherings at which worshippers met to eat another's flesh and to drink his blood. Details of such also were scarce and explanations were vague. Cults such as those of Cybele and of Bacchus, when left unchecked, could encourage incest, ritual fornication, and cannibalism. In theory, at least, Christianity might be another such sect. Whatever the case, there were rumors, which, as Virgil's *Aeneid* once reflected,[10] could spread rapidly and could not so easily be extinguished.

Christianity in the second century, as noted, was as yet unauthorized. It was a *religio illicita*. Despite that, Christians generally were not pursued. In a letter of AD 112 to the emperor Trajan, Pliny, the emperor's special imperial commissioner in Bithynia, recorded that, although he was a senator and lawyer and knew that Christianity was illegal, he did not know why.[11] He further remarked that, although Christians could be obstinate and intransigent, they were no more so than, for example, the swindling town councilors of Nicea and Nicomedia.[12] He then concluded that, with the emperor's agreement, he would not pursue Christians as he would criminals. If, however, they were publicly denounced and then refused both to recant and to worship the Roman gods, he would punish them.[13] If not denounced, it would then seem, Pliny was minded to leave Christians alone. Some twelve years later, in AD 124 or 125, Trajan's

10. Virgil, *Aeneid*, 4.173–97.

11. Pliny, *Letters*, 10.96.1.

12. Pliny, *Letters*, 10.31, and 10.33.

13. Pliny, *Letters*, 10.97.

successor, the emperor Hadrian (117–138), instructed Pliny both that people were not to seek out Christians and that the general practice of not admitting charges that were presented unsigned was to apply also in the case of Christians. He also mandated that a person, even when tried and then found guilty of having been a Christian, was yet to be pardoned, provided that the individual found guilty then demonstrated by engaging in a public act of worship of the imperial gods that he now no longer was a Christian. Further, Hadrian decreed that, if Christians were to be accused, Christians had to be accused in open court. Consequently, accusers were then required to bear the delay and any expenses of prosecution before a governor who generally attended a nearby assize perhaps once a year; and transparency and justice were seen to be promoted, any charges against an accused Christian now having to be heard before their accusers. Hadrian then added a significant rider: if the accusation failed, the accused, in accordance with the law of *calumnia*, which was especially aimed at preventing unwarranted persecutions, was then permitted to petition that the accuser should suffer substantial penalties for initiating vexatious litigation. For while Hadrian did hold that a Christian righty found guilty of doing anything contrary to the laws was to be punished in a way befitting the offense committed, he equally strongly maintained that anyone who levied accusations against Christians "merely for the sake of libeling them" was to suffer "heavier penalties, in accordance with his heinous guilt."[14] In the 110s and 120s, there seems to have been, therefore, an imperial self-confidence that extended, in practice, to tolerating, rather than pursuing, such critical minorities as Christians.

This decision by the second-century Greco-Roman Empire not to pursue Christians is further reflected in

14. Justin, *Apology*, 1.68.

the fact that between c.130 and 180 Christian apologists were able to write "open letters," formally addressed to the emperors, seeking to sway especially literate opinion that it might be more understanding of, and tolerant towards Christianity. Indeed, that Christian were not generally hunted down is further reflected in such debates as that in Rome between the Marcionite Apelles and the catholic Rhodo in AD 190. Rhodo had challenged Apelles to expound his faith, which Apelles did. There was, it therefore seems, at least in Rome at that time no general need for a Christian to hide his or her faith and religious attachment.

That said, in the second century we do find the *local* and *occasional* hunting down of Christians. Justin Martyr, for example, was denounced in 165 before the authorities in Rome by the Cynic Crescens, tried before the city prefect, Quintus Junius Rusticus, and, on refusing the demand to sacrifice, was condemned to death. This kind of pursuit of Christians, however, seems to have been local and occasional, and generally was instigated by individuals and trade associations, and not by imperial representatives.

In this generally tolerant era churches then sought to win converts, a practice generally followed neither by the synagogue nor by the cults of the empire. For the Jews mainly were racially exclusive and did not engage in proselytizing; and the cults did not see the need to convince a person of the reality of their own gods and the unreality of other people's gods, no one being either able or willing to say that this cult was true and that not, and everyone wishing rather to establish the peaceful co-existence of all cults.

The majority of those who then converted to Christianity were converts from a paganism that allowed a *mass* of gods, even in one individual's life, to an exclusive religion that believed in *one* God alone. Conversion to Christianity therefore required its converts to renounce all other gods and any practices associated with, or which might promote, the deities left behind. So Christians, both neophytes and those of long standing, withdrew their children from schools. For the capricious and, if understood literally, often immoral behavior of, for example, the Homeric gods featured in the curricula of local schools; and cultic observances punctuated school timetables. Tertullian described aspects of school life in north Africa in c.200. The cost of offerings to Minerva was taken from the fees of new pupils. Sacrifices frequently were offered. Prize-givings, when local dignitaries were present, were marked by cultic observances. Holidays were taken on the festivals of various gods.[15] By such inclusion of the cult in a school's life, even when such inclusion was only informal, a school modelled cultic practices. Indeed, in modelling such practices, a school provided a context in which the cult might be "caught" by its pupils, an altogether more subtle manner of "indoctrination" than any effected through teaching about a cult and its customs.

Christians further withdrew from wider society by, for example, avoiding buying meat in the markets, given the meat's provenance generally being a temple's sacrificial practices. This they did, even though it might have financial consequences for their town's economy. For their loyalty to the one God trumped their loyalty to their local town's economy.

Christians also increasingly refused to enter certain trades, even demanding that converts to Christianity who worked in any such "prohibited" trade should resign. If converts did not resign, they yet were to be very mindful that the Christian faith was to be sincerely and honestly lived daily, whatever the cost to their professional lives. So Christian converts who were painters, sculptors, and carvers were required not to undertake any commissions that might

15. Tertullian, *On Idolatry*, 10.

promote what to the Christian was idolatry. A soldier, who had not resigned from the army, was to commit to not killing. A gladiator was not to kill, a very costly injunction for both the gladiator and his owner. Equally, Christians were to choose not to enter the seemingly harmless trade associations or professional guilds; and those who were members of such associations and guilds, on becoming Christians, were expected to resign their membership of such. For these associations and guilds often performed various acts that had religious associations; and, insofar as such associations and guilds might act as funeral benefit societies, they frequently ensured that, on a member's death, cultic rites and rituals were enacted. The collateral cost for Christians of either not joining or resigning from such associations and guilds therefore included, but was not limited to, Christians separating themselves from their work-colleagues's friendship and support and a foregoing any financial and funeral help which these organizations traditionally afforded their members.

Further, Christians were not to sacrifice to the gods, even though not doing so would displease both the cult's priest and wider society. For the cultic priest, having paid for his office as priest, would have wished to make the most of his cult, encouraging people to make sacrifices. Wider society meanwhile, especially when threatened by natural calamity or hostile peoples, wished sacrifices to be offered by every member of society, both to appease any divine anger directed against it and, by its so honoring its gods, to become again the recipients of the gods's gift of peace. Yet, even when not threatened by natural calamity or hostile peoples, wider society wished sacrifices to be offered by as many members of society as possible. For, to varying degrees, it recognized that the very practices involved in offering sacrifices contributed to the up-building of communities. These practices included the careful allocation of the sacrificial animal, some parts being offered to the gods and other parts being given to the people. The thigh bones, sacrum and tail, for example, were burned for the gods, who, it was believed, feasted on the smoke. The entrails, once examined for signs of divine approval, were spit-roasted. The carcass was butchered, cooked, and consumed by the assembled people, either then and there, or taken elsewhere for eating later. So, the Hellenistic rite of animal sacrifice, as well as being a sharing of food with the gods, was, at one and the same time, also a sharing of food with the members of the local community, practices that resulted in the simultaneous strengthening of a community's relationship with its gods *and* between its participant members.

That Christians were not willing to offer or participate in such cultic sacrifices might well then have been seen, at the very least, as evidence that Christians were careless of their non-Christian neighbors, despite the assertions that Christians loved all their neighbors as themselves. Indeed, that Christians absented themselves from the sacrificial cult and its associated practices could also be read as signaling that Christians were those who opted out of even those everyday little behaviors and religious customs that made a community's daily living better together, and that especially enabled it "getting through" such liminal stages of its members' lives as births, marriages, and deaths.

More gravely, not being willing to engage in the empire's sacrificial cult might have been viewed as a sign of *sedition* and disloyalty to the province and the emperor. For not sacrificing amounted to undermining the empire's leadership in seeking the *pax Romana* for all the empire's peoples. What for Christian monotheism was an example of unwavering loyalty and faithfulness was for many a non-Christian a blatant example of selfish obstinacy, community disengagement, and unpatriotic intransigence.

Christian monotheism involved, however, not only the giving up of certain practices but also the taking up of others. One particular consequence of asserting belief in one God was asserting the *equality of all* before that one God. In second-century social order there was an absence of a clearly defined "merchant" class. Rather, there were relatively few benefactors and notables and many generally poor; and commonly the former paid for the amenities of civic life for the latter. For all that, within such a society the primary social distinction was not that between the "rich" and the "poor," but that between the "free" and the "enslaved." The second-century church largely mirrored that social stratification. That Clement of Alexandria [fl.180–200] chose to write the work *Whether the Rich Man May Be Saved?* presupposes the existence of some very rich Christian converts. The majority of Christians, however, were, in all probability, people of humbler origin, free men and women who might well have had at least some slaves. Some of these slaves, in all probability, also were Christians, people who along with the poor and the outcast had been attracted to Christianity because it offered them both a dignity, as children of God, and an otherworldly security, which this world denied them. In recognizing neither rich nor poor, free nor slave, but all one in Christ, the churches were therefore cutting across society's distinctions, even divisions of class and profession. They were challenging a concept of stability to which Greco-Roman society generally adhered.

The family in which the *paterfamilias* exercised almost complete authority was integral to society then; so too was the distinction between "free" and "slave." The church, however, struck at the family—a Christian mother was encouraged not to allow her non-Christian husband to rule unchecked over her children. Certain churches even allowed her to divorce such a husband. The church—even though there is early evidence of churches regularly stressing that being "one amongst equals" in the eyes of God should not be used to justify the breaking down of a household's conventional hierarchy[16]—was also perceived as undermining the separation of "free" from "slave." So, the church was thought by many in society to be striking at society's general stability. In short, the church's inclusivity, founded upon and informed by its belief in one God, cut across the social and economic homogeneity of second-century Greco-Roman society.

As noted, during the second century Christians seem not to have been pursued, neither systematically, nor continuously, nor for very long. When they were, some of the authorities before whom they were brought wished those accused of being Christians to deny their faith. So, for example, the proconsul, trying the arrested Bishop Polycarp of Smyrna in AD 156, repeatedly stated that, if Polycarp were to "curse Christ," he would be released;[17] and Pliny, in a letter of AD 112, reported to the emperor Trajan that he had tested that those accused of being Christians by requiring them to "curse Christ."[18] The majority, however, of the authorities before whom those accused of being Christians were brought did not demand a denial of faith. Rather, not appreciating the Christians's strict monotheism, they required them to recognize the Christian God as one god amongst many others. They sought Christian involvement in not only Christian worship but also the empire's cult, especially in its sacrificial system. Such they sought; and they were bemused when Christians resisted what they sought. This was partly because, as noted earlier, the empire

16. See 1 Corinthians 7:20–24.

17. *The Martyrdom of Polycarp*, 9.3.

18. Pliny, *Letters*, 10.96,5-6.

understood religion in terms of rites and rituals, not ideas and beliefs, and so could not understand why Christian ideas and beliefs stood in the way of their being willing to engage in a sacrificial rite.

The empire's bemusement was then deepened by the practices of the Jews and of those Christians, generically called gnostics. The Jews, the empire was aware, were willing to make a public act of sacrifice *for* the emperor, even though they were unwilling to sacrifice *to* the imperial cult; but Christians, perceived in some sense as an "offshoot" of Judaism, had no system of public sacrifices. Christians, the empire was told, did pray for the emperor; but the empire's officials could see no obvious proof of this. To people accustomed to seeing religion as a formal, public duty, involving *doing* something very overtly, being told that Christians *said* a prayer in the privacy of a house church must have seemed somewhat unsatisfactory, certainly in contrast with the *doing* involved in the Jews' public act of sacrificing for the emperor, if not wholly insufficient.

Some Christians, the empire was also aware, whilst they did not step forward to offer to sacrifice to the gods of the cults, did not, when required to sacrifice, refuse to sacrifice. What the empire did not appreciate was that these Christians, gnostics, unlike catholics, were of the opinion that the world of matter and of history was completely inconsequential. Some of these therefore abstained as rigorously as possible from the inconsequential world of matter and history. These gnostics would never sacrifice to the gods of the cults. Other gnostics, however, also believing that the world of matter and history was completely inconsequential, maintained therefore that they could be so lax in their relationship to matter that any historical act, sacrificing to the gods included, could be done, without that act, in any way whatsoever, affecting their salvation.

Whereas catholic Christians would have viewed sacrificing to the gods of the imperial cults as committing the unforgiveable sin of crucifying again their already-crucified Savior,[19] this latter group of gnostic Christians saw such an act as not even insignificant, but void of value. When faced with the readiness of such gnostic Christians, when asked, to sacrifice, civic authorities would not have easily understood why *all* Christians would not, when asked, offer sacrifices to the gods of the empire.

That incomprehension, especially when put alongside both a concentration upon rites and rituals rather than beliefs and syncretic, pluralist theologies, may help to explain, though not excuse, why prosecuting officials and their supporters sometimes forsook persuasion and took to threats in their attempt to elicit a sacrifice to the gods of their cults.

Vibia Perpetua, a twenty-two year old with an infant child at her breast, came from a religiously divided family. She, her brother, Dinocrates, and her slave, Felicitas, were Christian catechumens. Her father, mother, aunt, and other brother were pagans. In AD 202 or AD 203, Perpetua was brought before the procurator Hilarianus in Carthage and ordered to make a sacrifice.[20] Pleas and threats ensued. Yet not even the pleas nor the threats of her father, the *paterfamilias*—whose will, pagans assumed, was always to be obeyed by his children—resulted in the desired obedience and sacrifice. So Perpetua and Felicitas were killed.

Some forty-six years earlier, in AD 156, Polycarp, the eighty-six-year-old bishop of Smyrna, although widely held in high esteem, was charged with being a Christian. On the way from the farm house in which he was found to the amphitheater in Smyrna where he was to be killed, the arresting police chief sought to persuade Polycarp to

19. See Hebrews 6:4–6.

20. *Martyrdom of Perpetua and Felicitas*, 1–21.

do something, anything, which might have saved his life. People searched for a convenient form of words that might have spared Polycarp. They suggested that he said, "away with the atheists," by which *they* meant "away with the Christians who denied the gods of the empire." He complied, saying, "away with the atheists," by which *he* meant, "away with the pagans, who denied the one, true God of the Christians." Subsequent demands of Polycarp he would not grant; and so he was killed.

Even allowing for the possibility that such accounts as these of Perpetua's and Polycarp's martyrdoms were written in such a manner as to encourage resistance to both smooth and harsh words which sought to lead Christians into ways that all Christians should resist, these accounts do suggest the degree of incomprehension on the part of pagan officials, demanding sacrifices, when faced with what they saw as Christian obstinacy. What Christians believed or did not believe, especially as "belief" or "faith" was thought to be the lowest form of cognition by those brought up on classical Greek philosophy, was of little concern. What was of concern to the local officials was a gesture, literally a gesture of honor to the cult, and an acceptance of a widely held religious tradition. One can almost hear their plaintiff cry, "We are not asking you to forsake the worship of your god. We are simply asking you to honor our gods as well." For, in short, the official powers wanted peace and stability, not martyrs for a faith.

It was in this wider context that Christians began to write "apologies," explaining and, to some extent, defending their worship and way of life. Their themes already are outlined in Bishop Polycarp's conversation with the proconsul of Asia in the amphitheater in Smyrna in AD 156. In Polycarp's looking "up to heaven and [saying], away with the atheists," he was highlighting both the Christians's commitment to the one God of the Gospels—"heaven," to which Polycarp lifted his eyes, being a frequent circumlocution for "God"—and their resistance to that "atheism" that denied the one true God in its exchanging the worship of the Creator for that of creation, as embodied in the cultic statues before which sacrifices were offered. In offering the proconsul an opportunity to learn the doctrines of Christianity, Polycarp was seeking both to be open and transparent, not secretive, and to give the lie to the rumors that Christians engaged in immorality and cannibalism. In telling the proconsul that Christians "have been taught to render honor, as is proper, if it does not hurt [Christians], to princes and authorities appointed by God,"[21] Polycarp was outlining the very nuanced position that Christians then were minded to maintain towards the imperial and civic powers of the empire. In short, the main themes that the Apologists sought to address were the very same topics that Christians—be they the bishop of an ancient see or a young, breast-feeding mother in Carthage—could find themselves addressing in their daily life.

QUESTIONS FOR REFLECTION AND DISCUSSION

1. Given that to many minds good governance, effective administration, better finances, and enhanced infrastructure generally lead to a state's peace and prosperity, to what extent was Celsus correct when he maintained that whatever Christians receive in this world, they receive from the state alone?

2. In what sense, if any, may people properly speak of the God of Christianity being wrathful?

21. Eusebius, *Ecclesiastical History*, 6.15.18–25. See also Romans 13:1–4.

3. What place in religion is there for the practice of propitiating, or appeasing, the divine?

4. Some early Apologists saw the empire as the enemy of the church, while others recognized that even a non-Christian emperor could be, and often was, a minster of God. How may these very different perspectives contribute to the thinking of contemporary churches as they contemplate how better to relate to their governments and peoples?

5. How radical should conversion to Christianity be? Should, for example, Christian parents insist upon their children being educated only in a church school, or, indeed, only in a school of a particular Christian denomination? Or, in what ways should members of the armed forces, upon converting to Christianity, reconsider their position?

2

SIX GREEK CHRISTIAN APOLOGISTS

ALONGSIDE A NUMBER OF fragments of Quadratus, Melito of Sardis, and Apollinaris of Hierapolis, found mainly in Eusebius of Caesarea's *Ecclesiastical History*, the letters of five Greek Christian Apologists and an anonymous *Letter to Diognetus* have survived. The five attributable letters are those of Aristides, Justin Martyr, Tatian, Athenagoras, and Theophilos of Antioch. These letter writers were aware that the Christianity faith, which for a while had shown signs of difference in thought and practice amongst its adherents, was then becoming increasingly distinct in thought and practice both from the synagogue and from Hellenistic life and culture. Indeed, they were aware that Christianity's particular beliefs and practices were, at times, even at odds with other religious beliefs or practices, and so were eliciting comments, often critical, from the cities of the empire in which Christians were. To such comments these Apologists responded. They sought, as Aristides explained, to examine differing philosophical schools and religions, Christianity included, "in order that [their readers] might understand which of [these schools and religions contained] the truth concerning God, and which . . . error."[1] They concerned themselves with defending the beliefs, worship, and daily life of Christians. Further, they applied themselves to advocating these. For, for them, what was at stake was "the truth concerning God," a truth that they saw as being not theoretical but theological, one that made for not just debate but a truthful way of living. Not surprisingly then, integral to these Apologists defending Christianity was their engaging in Christian mission.

Certainly, in prosecuting their defenses, the Apologists aimed to explain and justify Christian beliefs and practices. Some, such as Theophilos of Antioch, did so primarily by citing scriptural texts. Others, such as Aristides and the anonymous writer of the *Letter to Diognetus*, it would seem, rather worked with the thesis that "deeds spoke louder than words"; "louder" not in the sense that they thought that texts were somewhat inaudible and so less cogent, but in the sense that they were of the mind that the truth often was more readily discernible through a life lived than through a text heard, especially when the text was that of an alien religious tradition. Aristides and the anonymous letter writer therefore centered their defense upon descriptions of the lifestyle of Christians. In some ways their argument was not so different from that of some philosophers of the time—the truth, both commonly held, was especially demonstrated by holy living.

In one way, however, their argument differed greatly from that of many contemporary philosophers. For these Apologists attended to the lives of, not an élite, let alone a philosophical élite, but people of all conditions, estates,

1. Aristides, *Apology*, 3.

and standings. To their minds, the ordinariness of a Christian's life and the extraordinariness of a Christian's way of life only strengthened their defense, especially their defense before those who never had nor would read the Christian scriptures but might be inclined to read the lives of Christians, as if these lives were "the Christian scriptures." So, using thinking not dissimilar from that in the apostle Paul's image of "treasure in earthen vessels . . . [which] show that the transcendent power belongs to God and not to [mere humans],"[2] these Apologists highlighted divine truth evidenced in ordinary, often lowly, and always fallible members of second-century society. Just as the scriptural texts employed, for example, by a Theophilos of Antioch pointed beyond themselves to God, so the holiness of ordinary lives, sustained even in the most unholy of situations, pointed beyond ordinary humanity to the holy One.

Yet, however the Apologists chose to mount their defense, whether through texts cited or holiness of living, they sought thereby to display Christianity's attractiveness, and so they found themselves commending Christianity, proselytizing by any other name. Yet such "proselytizing" was a consequence, not the cause, of their describing what it meant to be a Christian in the mid-to-late second century.

Four of these Apologies were addressed to emperors. That said, it is unlikely that their intended readers were these emperors. For only exceptionally did emperors then tend to deal with matters that affected only small segments of the population, and, generally speaking, Christianity was not then viewed as one such matter. Rather, their intended readers probably were curious, literate, hopefully persuadable Greeks and those Christians who were able and ready to learn how to engage critically with the cults of the wider Greco-Roman world and the culture and practices of their

2. 2 Corinthians 4:7.

neighborhoods, in a defense of their faith. In that sense, these letters were "open" letters. In two cases, however, the apologetic letters were addressed specifically to two individuals, a certain Diognetus and a certain Autolycus. Even then, however, it may be supposed that the readers of these two letters were not limited to these two individuals.

Many of the Apologists were concerned to meet such charges as their being "atheists," their alleged engagement in immoral practices, such as sexual promiscuity and cannibalism, their being followers of a "Johnny come lately" religion, and their being disloyal to the empire and its emperors.

Severally and together these Apologists argued that they were not atheists. For they believed in one god. If they were "atheists," they were such only because, being monotheists, they necessarily denied all gods but the one true God.

Severally and together, the Apologists insisted that Christians were neither sexually promiscuous nor cannibals. They all cited the scriptural basis for their morality, drawing especially on the Decalogue and the Sermon on the Mount, two sets of texts chosen in part because of their explicit condemnation of adultery and murder, and in part because by the early 170s the church's emerging canon of Scripture—and so the rule by which Christians judged themselves and were willing to be judged—recognized as authoritative the Hebrew Scriptures, the four Gospels, and thirteen letters of the apostle Paul. Many of the Apologists also described the high morality evident in Christian daily living. Justin Martyr went even further than that, describing the rite of the Eucharist, hoping thereby to counter the false inferences drawn by non-Christians from their misunderstandings of both the dominical injunction to love one another and the eucharistic practice of feeding on the body of Christ.

All but one of the Apologists recognized that Christ came late in time, but asserted nevertheless that Christ had come as had been foretold centuries before by Hebrew prophets, more ancient and much more trustworthy witnesses than any Greek philosopher, dramatist, or poet.

The exception to the above was Theophilos of Antioch. He was exceptional only in that, at best, he only *alluded* to Christ, and so, not explicitly mentioning Christ, limited his argument to maintaining that the truth which Christianity owned had been given first and most reliably by God's Word (*Logos*) to Moses and to the Hebrew prophets, upon whom any others who spoke the truth were wholly dependent.

While acknowledging, on the grounds of monotheism, that Christians absented themselves from the empire's pagan cults, the majority of Apologists affirmed their loyalty to the empire, acknowledging that Christians also benefitted from its peace. Some Apologists even assured both the emperors of their prayers and the empire of their contribution to its well-being in and through their keeping all its reasonable laws. In this regard, however, when the Apologists differed in their views, they sometimes differed very markedly. Tatian, for example, was adamantly *contra mundum*, opposed to the world, while Athenagoras, even allowing for his literary style, was almost obsequious in his assurances of loyalty to the emperors Marcus Aurelius and Commodus.

Integral to the arguments of these Apologists are the thoughts that God, through his Word, is the Maker of all things, and that the Scriptures are reliable, God-given resources for discerning both the truth and how to live with probity. These thoughts helped churches more generally to undermine the opinions of such groups as gnostic Christians, who questioned, if not denied, God's role in making and sustaining the contingent world of particularity, and

the followers of Marcion (d. c.160), who rejected both
the Hebrew Scriptures and much of the New Testament
as vehicles for the Christian God's self-revelation. For the
Apologists asserted the goodness of all that was made.
They emphasized the importance of history, important
both as that in and through which God had revealed himself and as that to be hallowed daily by both individuals
and communities living Christ-like lives. They also maintained Scripture's role in enabling a community to discern
orthodoxy and orthopraxis.

That said, it is not clear that the Apologists generally
targeted such groups as the gnostics and Marcionites. If anything, in most cases, the Apologists inflicted "collateral" rather than "directly targeted" damage on them. Justin Martyr's
understanding of the creative role of the one, gracious God
and Theophilos of Antioch's sense of the good God whose
creation was seen to be good, even allowing for Justin's and
Theophilos's slight differences in thinking, are examples of
theological positions that stood in contrast with Marcion's
two gods—the god of the Hebrew Scriptures, a lower Demiurge, or Craftsman, who created the world, and the su-
preme God, the God of grace and redeeming love, first made
known by Christ. Moreover, given that between the thinking
of Marcion and that of gnostics then there was a kinship, albeit not an identity—for Marcion refrained from associating
himself with the gnostics in their identifying the Demiurge
with the principle of evil—Justin Martyr's and Theophilos of
Antioch's understandings of the Creator God also implicitly
criticized the gnostics's theological dualism and their consequential disregard for matter's worth and people's proper role
as material beings within the wider creation.

To the writings of these Apologists we now turn. We
do so, mindful, however, of the facts that they were less
members of a single movement and more individuals with

generally common concerns, that their answers to their common concerns are different, even at times conflicting, and that their writings are not, therefore, such that it is possible to trace within them either a natural development or evolution.

ARISTIDES'S *APOLOGY*

Aristides's *Apology* is carefully studied in style. The religious ideas and practices that it describes and advocates are those that reflect a time when churches, whilst no longer under the wing of the synagogue, were not obviously hesitant in taking the synagogue occasionally under their wing. Their ethics evidence strong continuity with Hellenistic-Jewish ethics. So, caring for the poor, ransoming prisoners, and burying the dead are given as characteristic virtues of both Judaism and Christianity.[3] The mid-second-century Jewish thought that the beauty of the world was created for Israel is slightly altered by Aristides. It is here presented as having been created for Christians, although still so presented within a wider understanding in which God's creation is for humanity's sake. Further, the then Jewish practice of classifying the human race according to religion is employed: "there are," Aristides wrote, "four races of humanity . . . barbarians, Greeks, Jews and Christians."[4] These four races Aristides then examined and evaluated as to how far each "possessed the truth concerning God."[5] Aristides's conclusions were that the barbarians were to be criticized for falling away from the truth, pursuing the desires of their own

3. Aristides, *Apology*, 14–15. See also 2 Enoch 51.1 and The Sibylline Oracles, 3.

4. Aristides, *Apology*, 2.

5. Aristides, *Apology*, 3.

minds, and worshipping creation rather than its Creator;[6] the Greeks were to be rebuked for introducing gods whose lives were corrupt, something that then gave credence to their devotees's corrupt lives;[7] and the Egyptians were described as "more evil and ignorant than all the peoples upon the earth"[8] in that they had given the name of "god" even to "beasts which are soulless,"[9] an error for which they were doubly culpable as they clearly had not heeded the force of the Hellenistic-Jewish apologetic, based on such psalms as Psalm 115, which contrasted the sovereign God in heaven with the manufactured idols on earth, made with hands and feet, but yet unable to touch and walk. In comparison, the Jews were treated quite favorably. They, it was acknowledged, worshipped the one God and lived highly moral lives. The main criticism levelled against them was a traditional criticism, that through their ceremonies they served angels and not God alone.[10] Aristides also criticized Jews in a quasi-creedal statement that spoke of the church's Lord as "he [who] was crucified by the Jews."[11]

6. Aristides, *Apology*, 7. See also Romans 1:21–25.

7. Aristides, *Apology*, 11.

8. Aristides, *Apology*, 12.

9. Aristides, *Apology*, 12. Amongst philosophers then the Stoics perhaps most sharply distinguished humans from animals, seeing the former as significantly more dignified, on account of their possessing a rational soul and having free will. Against this philosophical background, Aristides's critique of the Egyptians's deifying animals only highlights the depths to which the Egyptians have fallen.

10. Aristides, *Apology*, 14. See also Colossians 2:16–18 and The Preaching of Peter, quoted in Origin's *Commentary on John*, 13:17, where Jews are treated courteously but criticized for worshipping angels and for ritually observing the months and the new moons, even whilst also knowing one God.

11. Aristides, *Apology*, 2. See also Justin Martyr, *Dialogue with Trypho*, 16.

Aristides's purpose, as noted, was primarily to assess where truth lay, and not to counter, as some other Apologists sought to do, the traditional charges brought against Christians. That said, there are hints that Aristides was not unaware of these charges. Not in a systematic way, as Aristides might have done had he chosen to respond explicitly to the specific charges made against Christians, but in a clear manner, in language that echoed that of the Decalogue, he described the Christian way of life, emphasizing that Christians did not commit adultery.[12] He criticized the Greek gods and their devotees for being cannibals and for defiling their mothers and sisters.[13] He pointed out that Christians, though critical of the world, did not wholly disown it. For "the world stands by reason of the prayers offered by Christians."[14] This was to fall short of other Apologists, who promised to pray for the emperor as God's appointed ruler, and who insisted that the reasonable laws of the empire were to be obeyed. It was, however, to suggest that the high morality that Christians sought to exhibit was to be exhibited not only in inter-Christian relationships, but also in Christian relationships with wider society.

Given Aristides's inheritance from the Hellenistic synagogue and relatively favorable portrayal of second-century Judaism, favorable certainly in comparison with his portrayal of his three other "human races," some scholars have dated his *Apology* to a time "well before 132."[15] That date certainly would accord with Eusebius's having written that Aristides's *Apology* was addressed to Hadrian, the emperor from 117–138.[16] The Syriac translation of the *Apology*,

12. Aristides, *Apology*, 15.

13. Aristides, *Apology*, 9.

14. Aristides, *Apology*, 16.

15. Grant, *The Greek Apologists*, 39.

16. Eusebius, *Ecclesiastical History*, 4.3.3.

discovered only in 1889, maintains, however, that the *Apology* was addressed to emperor Antoninus Pius, during the early years of his reign [138–161], possibly during an unrecorded visit to Smyrna. If that is the case, that would suggest a date of composition in the early 140s, maybe c.145.[17] This date would not be too late to account for the Apologist's generally positive portrayal of Hellenistic Judaism. Yet this date would also be late enough to avoid Aristides embarrassing the very person whom he could hardly afford to embarrass. The emperor Hadrian had a "favorite" of the name of Antinous, a young man who, in 130, drowned in the Nile, and whom Hadrian then deified. Aristides clearly wished to win the support of the emperor to whom he addressed his *Apology* for Christianity; and it would seem unlikely therefore that the emperor to whom he wrote to commend Christianity was Hadrian when in his *Apology* Aristides included both a criticism of homosexuality[18] and an assertion that human beings cannot be divine since they have beginnings and ends.[19] It seems better therefore to date the *Apology* after the death of the emperor Hadrian. To do so would further tally with the fact that even implied criticism of the divinized Antinous by Apologists was generally voiced only from Antoninus Pius's time and onwards. It would also avoid the rather over-complicated suggestion that the Greek version of the *Apology* was delivered during

17. So Harris and Robinson, *The Apology of Aristides*, Introduction, 2.

18. Aristides, *Apology*, 17 [Syriac version]. See also Aristides, *Apology*, 9 [Greek version] and parallels in Aristides, *Apology*, 8 [Syriac version] where Aristides, addressing the emperor, criticized Greeks for becoming adulterers and passionate men, in imitating of their gods. See also Aristides, *Apology*, 13 [Syriac and Greek versions], where it is argued that, if the Greek laws are just, their gods are unjust in that, amongst other things, their gods commit sodomy.

19. Aristides, *Apology*, 12.

Hadrian's reign and that a revised version of the *Apology*, the Syriac version, was delivered only after Hadrian's death.[20]

Aristides's commendation of Christianity and his consequent criticism of other faiths and cults were intended as a relatively dispassionate inquiry into where truth was to be found. In keeping with that intention Aristides increasingly failed. He mentioned aspects of Christian faith as though they were very familiar to his non-Christian audience. He referred to angels as though they were part and parcel of not only Jewish but also general religious discussion. Evangelistically, he encouraged all to accept Christian teaching, "the gateway of light," that each might "anticipate Jesus Christ's dread judgement, which would come upon all."[21] Increasingly a dispassionate presentation gave way to an advocating the Christians's case, and then to a convinced Christian's setting forth the faith that was his, and that he wished would become that of his readers.

That said, it cannot be said that Aristides's argument was unique. His faith was in continuity with the Christianity to be found in *1 Clement* and Polycarp's *Letter to the Philippians*, and was an anticipation of the *Letter to Diognetus*, for whose author also Christianity was not simply to be discussed but also to be commended and lived.

LETTER TO DIOGNETUS

Who the author of the first ten chapters of the *Letter to Diognetus* was is not known.[22] Equally, who the recipient of

20. Grant. *The Greek Apologists,* 39, 45.

21. Aristides, *Apology,* 17.

22. It is assumed that chapters 11–12 of the *Letter to Diognetus,* with their difference in style and content from those of chapters 1–10, are by another author. See Ehrman, *The Apostolic Fathers,* Vol. 2, 123–24; and Jefford, *The Epistle to Diognetus,* 43–51.

the letter was is unknown. All that can reasonably be noted is that he went by the name of Diognetus, was given the title "most Excellent," and was treated with appropriate respect.

The elegantly written work is similar to Aristides's *Apology*, but not dependent upon it. Like Aristides's work, it blends Hellenism and Judaism. It uses such apologetics as are to be found in Psalm 115, in the Wisdom of Solomon,[23] and in the Sibylline Oracles.[24] Its understanding of creation also is anthropocentric, the world being understood as having been made for humanity's sake.

In other respects it is dissimilar from Aristides's *Apology*. It views Christians as having taken the place of Jews as those who were responsible for representing all people to God. It portrays Christians as the world's "soul."[25] In its portrayal, not only, however, has the *role* of Christians in the world changed. So too has their *theology*. Whatever theological accord there had been between Christians and Jews, little was here acknowledged. The cult of Christians, not that of the Torah, is viewed as the true cult; their gospel is understood as the fulfilment of the Hebrew prophecies; and the divine Logos, the agent of creation, late in coming as Christ, is their and the world's savior. Indeed, to the letter writer's mind, so much has Christianity's association with Judaism been severed that the letter writer felt justified in writing that, on the one hand, Christians rightly distanced themselves from Jewish thinking and practice and, on the other, that Jews treated Christians as "foreigners and enemies."[26] So far had amity given way to enmity.

Dating the anonymous letter is challenging. It could have been written any time between 130 and 190. Its use,

23. Wisdom of Solomon 13–15.

24. The Sibylline Oracles, 3.

25. *To Diognetus*, 6. See also Philo, *Embassy* 1.3–4.

26. *To Diognetus* 5.

however, of Hellenistic-Jewish apologetic arguments, its decisive theological break from Jewish thinking, especially in the prominence that it gives to the Logos, the Word of God, in its explanation as to why the Son came late in time, and its employing neither Euhemerist arguments, namely the referring of myths to historical bases, nor other argument often used by later Apologists against beliefs concerning pagan gods, together suggest a date of c.150,[27] possibly in Alexandria.[28]

The Letter's agenda is set out in the opening chapter where the Letter's recipient is reported as being eager to learn about Christians and their religion. Indeed, he is portrayed as asking, "who is the God in whom Christians trust, and how do they worship God?"[29] These two questions were asked because Diognetus is reported as having noticed the Christians's detachment from the world, their disregard for death, and their rejection of both the gods of the Greeks and the cult of the Jews. Diognetus is also described as being curious about what he saw as the novelty of Christianity, a theme that he saw as raising significant questions concerning the authenticity of the religion of the Christians. In this Diognetus was clearly echoing the then widely held opinion that what was new was deemed to be suspect, whilst what was ancient, and tested by time, was seen as genuine. Diognetus also is pictured as intrigued by the "affection which Christians have for one another."[30]

At one level Diognetus seemed to be interested in religious questions. At another level, however, he also seemed to be interested in very practical, even political

27. See Holmes, *The Apostolic Fathers*, 293. See also Jefford, *The Epistle to Diognetus*, 15–29.

28. See Jefford, *Epistle to Diognetus*, 28–29.

29. *To Diognetus*, 1.

30. *To Diognetus*, 1. See also 1 John 4:7.

questions, an understandable interest when it is remembered that religious issues in the second century often had political overtones. For, for anyone, Christians included, to show disdain towards the particular beliefs and practices of those amongst whom someone lived, especially through a refusal to be involved in the imperial cult, led to questions being asked as to whether, in not supporting the imperial *status quo*, that person was in any way acting seditiously. Further, Christians's loving one another, a mutual love highlighted by their distancing themselves from and even their disregarding the empire's shared cultural and religious life, raised suspicions that they were members of secret, closed societies. In times of peace, therefore, Christians might be perceived to be anti-social, and so undermining of shared public life; and, in times of war, the self-same individuals might be viewed to be provocatively disloyal to the universal call for imperial unity in the face of an external military threat.

That said, and if, as suggested, the Letter was written in c.150, when the persecution of Christians was hardly sustained, Diognetus's questions are, in one sense, less pressing in their need to be answered and perhaps rather more theoretical, less requiring a defense against the possibility of being pursued and prosecuted for either sedition or membership of secret, destabilizing societies, and more the result of Diognetus's intellectual curiosity. For the letter writer, however, the answers to the questions were less than theoretical answers and certainly were more than those necessary to meet his reader's curiosity. As with anyone making a defense, the letter writer wanted his arguments to be heard, and heard fairly. So he asked his reader to lay aside all bias and to adopt the perspective of an individual "who is to hear a new story."[31] This letter writer, however,

31. *To Diognetus*, 2.1.

it would seem, wanted more than that. As for Aristides in his *Apology* to Antoninus Pius, so for this letter writer, the desired outcome extended beyond his receiving a fair hearing, beyond the letter's recipient's eventually being better informed about Christianity, and reached towards Diognetus's finally becoming a fellow Christian. So, even before beginning any defense of Christianity, Diognetus's correspondent *prayed* that he might speak with good effect and that Diognetus might be edified, build up to *know* God, and not just to *know about* God and the Christian religion.[32] Indeed, at the end of chapter 10, he expressed his hope that Diognetus, having come to know the Father, "will see that God lives in heaven, . . . will begin to speak of God, . . . will love and admire those being punished for their refusal to deny God, . . . and will condemn the world's deceit and error."[33] The anonymous letter writer was eager both that he would not be persecuted for having written in favor of the one God and against the world's many gods, and that he might be the instrument by which Diognetus became a Christian. His argument, therefore, sought a change of heart in the letter's recipient towards both Christians and their God. In short, the *Letter to Diognetus*, whilst being a defense of Christianity, is also an instrument of Christian mission.

JUSTIN MARTYR—*APOLOGIES* AND *DIALOGUE WITH TRYPHO*

In comparison with Aristides, and especially with the writer to Diognetus, we know much about Justin. The son of Priscus and grandson of Bacchus, gentile Greek settlers, Justin was born in Flavia Neapolis, modern day Nablus, in

32. *To Diognetus*, 1; See also *To Diognetus*, 2.1.

33. *To Diognetus*, 10.7.

Samaria. As a young man he left home in order to engage upon a religious quest to find God, and, on finding God, to live accordingly.

His quest, interestingly, did not begin with either the Jewish or Samaritan thinking of his birthplace. Rather, it started with his exploring firstly the philosophy of the Stoics, then that of the Peripatetics, then that of the Pythagoreans, and then that of the Platonists. In time, however, on the seashore at Ephesus, Justin met an elderly Christian, whose background seems to have been that of a "godfearer," someone sympathetic to Judaism, and who was also reasonably acquainted with Platonism. In discussion with the young Justin, this elderly Christian criticized, slightly unfairly, the Platonic theme of reminiscence.[34] He insisted upon the role of the Holy Spirit in enabling God's communion with the human soul. Then, having highlighted the Spirit's particular role in God's self-unveiling, he pointed to the writings of the Hebrew prophets who, he maintained, being divinely inspired, properly directed their readers to the knowledge of the true God. It was, however, only subsequently, on witnessing the constancy of Christians even when faced with the threat of being killed if they did not renounce their faith that Justin committed himself to Christianity. The combination of truth and moral earnestness Justin found compelling. That said, he never abandoned his earlier respect for Stoic ethics and Platonism, but accepted Christianity as the complete revelation of the truth as adumbrated in Stoicism and Platonism.

Eventually Justin settled in Rome. There he established a school, disputed with both the adherents of the locally expounded philosophies, the proponents of various forms of gnostic thinking and the followers of Marcion,

34. See Plato, *Phaedrus*, 249C–D.

and, according to Eusebius of Caesarea,[35] concurrently wrote eight books. Of the surviving manuscripts which Eusebius attributed to Justin, three are indisputably by him, two Apologies and a Dialogue with the Jew Trypho, works dated, respectively to c.155, c.161, and c.160.

Some five years later, Justin, along with six companions, was beheaded. The Apologist Tatian, one of Justin's pupils, laid the blame for Justin's summons to trial at the feet of the Cynic Crescens, against whom Justin had written, and who had denounced Justin before the authorities; and *The Acts of Justin and His Companions* records both Justin's trial in Rome before the city prefect, Quintus Junius Rusticus, and Justin's refusal to sacrifice to the imperial gods. His martyrdom was then inevitable.

In his writings Justin argued from the Hebrew Scriptures for the truth of Christianity. He posited that the truth fully revealed and lived in Christianity could in part be glimpsed in Stoic ethics and Platonic philosophy—Christianity was indeed the true philosophy; but there had been "Christians before Christ." Socrates, for example, was one such.[36] He further held that, as Christianity was not wholly antithetical to the philosophical systems of the time, Christianity was not diametrically opposed to the state.

Justin therefore was loyal to the empire, holding it and its emperor in his prayers. Yet he was not uncritically loyal to it. When and where he judged its laws to be unjust, he commented. So, for example, he criticized those laws that sought to hinder a Christian's worship; and he spoke out again those that forbad people's reading the books of Hystaspes and the Sibyl prophets, writings that possibly promoted the idea that the Messiah would come as the head of armies from

35. Eusebius, *Ecclesiastical History*, 4.18.

36. Justin, *Apology*, 1.46.

the east, forces led by Rome's enemies.[37] Noteworthy here is Justin's commitment to justice *for* all and *from* all. Despite his general disapproval of Judaism, he spoke out against laws as they unjustly effected Jews; and, in attributing the promulgation of these laws to "wicked demons,"[38] so implying that the promulgators of the laws were demon-possessed, he rather obviously called upon the imperial lawmakers henceforth to rule with righteousness.

Certainly when compared with Aristides Justin appears to have been somewhat more conciliatory. He seems to have been more ready to engage in discussion. It might therefore be supposed that his tone was more theoretical and less applied, as might befit a school in Rome then. Such a supposition would not, however, be right. His writing is conciliatory, but, when thought necessary, it does not shy away from hard words. As noted above, Justin did not hesitate to rebuke those who enacted laws that, to Justin's mind, worked unjustly against Jews. He did not hesitate from telling Emperor Antoninus Pius, to whom he addressed his First Apology, that, if he continued in his injustice towards Christians, even though he was the emperor, he would have to face divine judgement for his wrong ways. Nor was Justin unaware of the risks that he faced as he sought to defend Christianity. He knew that Christianity was not simply an interesting topic solely to be discussed, but a truth to be lived, and, if necessary, for which to be willing to be martyred, as indeed he was.

---

37. See Origen, *Against Celsus*, 2.29 and The Sibylline Oracles, 5.415.

38. Justin, *Apology*, 1.44.

TATIAN

Tatian [fl.160–180], a pupil, but not a disciple of Justin—indeed, he was to become an uncompromising opponent of Justin's thinking—was born an "Assyrian," of pagan parents, east of the Euphrates, in the area between the Roman Empire and Parthia. In time, like his future tutor, he too travelled west, in order to explore the philosophies of the Greco-Roman world. Eventually, having visited Athens, he settled in Rome. There he initially was initiated into one of the many mystery cults of the time; but, as he himself recorded, he soon became disillusioned with the cult. Then, influenced by Justin Martyr, he embraced Christianity. He was impressed by the assertion that the prophecies of the Hebrew Scriptures found their fulfilment in Christian times. He was convinced that Christianity was not a novel invention but a very venerable religion of great antiquity. He was attracted by Christianity's universality, its being open to all, irrespective of wealth, gender, or age, its consistency and its straightforwardness. He found in Christianity a robust basis for critiquing both pagan religions and Roman law and governance. Indeed, he saw in Christianity not just a basis for critiquing, but for condemning Roman law and governance. Unlike Aristides and his teacher Justin, Tatian would not grant that Roman law and governance, even though perhaps open to criticism in certain aspects, had yet been helpful in allowing the spreading of Christianity; and, whereas his teacher Justin argued that the fact that legal codes accepted in one place were often unacceptable in another prompted the reasonable observer to critique aspects of Roman law and governance, Tatian, Justin pupil, saw that same fact as requiring the same reasonable observer to dismiss completely Roman law and governance.

Tatian's *Address to the Greeks*, which, because of the legacy of the thought of Tatian's tutor Justin [died 165] still evident in it, is usually dated somewhat indefinitely between 155 and 165,[39] was called by Eusebius of Caesarea "the best and most useful of all" Tatian's works.[40] Yet, for all the influence of Justin, Tatian's *Address* is somewhat hesitant when addressing Christianity. It stresses the role of the Logos in the act of creation; but it fails to make explicit mention of "Jesus," "Christ," or "Christians," possibly because it is hesitant to affirm matter, and so, by extension, the humanity of Christ and of his followers, and their respective histories.[41] Certainly, Tatian's *Address* so emphasizes the role of the Logos as a Demiurge, an intermediary between God, on the one hand, and the created order of humans and angels on the other, that, if not dividing God

39. Cf. Grant, *The Greek Apologists*, 113–15, who suggested that Tatian's *Address* was probably written not long after the end of 176. For Grant noted the reference in Tatian's *Address*, 19 to some philosophers each receiving "600 gold coins a year from the Roman emperor." This Grant then connected with the Roman emperor's establishing in the autumn of 176 four professorships of philosophy and one of rhetoric, each at a cost of 400 gold coins a year. He then stated that Tatian's reference to the higher, or as Grant wrote, "exaggerated" figure of 600 gold pieces apiece a year, as opposed to the actual 400 gold pieces apiece a year, "must be due to envy" on Tatian's part. In view of the influence of the thinking of Justin [d. 165] upon that of his pupil Tatian in the latter's *Address*, of the significant difference between the two sums of gold coins mentioned, which cannot be so easily explained, at least in this case, by an unevidenced "must," and of the likelihood that Tatian broke away from the church in 172, after which, as Irenaeus related [*Against the Heresies*, 1.28.1], Tatian "composed his own peculiar type of doctrine," doctrine rather different from that found in the *Address*, the earlier date of composition, even if it is a decade rather than a precise year, is to be preferred.

40. Eusebius, *Ecclesiastical Histories*, 4.29.

41. See Head, "Tatian's Christology and Its Influence in the Composition of the Diatessaron."

from matter, it separates God from matter, and so down-played matter's importance.[42]

Such a down-playing of the importance of matter was, however, but the beginning of such. In time, most likely some time after Justin's death in 165, Tatian returned to the east. There, in Mesopotamia, he founded his own school, and began to teach an increasingly extreme form of ascetical Christianity. He held that the Christian ethics taught by his mentor Justin were not sufficiently distinct from the moral-ity of the Greco-Roman city-states of the 170s. Certainly, as reported by Irenaeus, Tatian then maintained that marriage was nothing short of corruption and fornication,[43] a theme foreshadowed in his treatment of marriage in his earlier *Ad-dress*, with its harsh criticism of even sex within marriage; and he insisted on not eating animals. It is true that some very early Christians had sometimes advocated celibacy[44] and others had deemed a vegetarian diet to be proper.[45] Yet Tatian's ethical demands far exceeded such early Christian ethical demands; and, unlike his mentor Justin, he definitely did not permit different ethical practices for different Christ-ians, provided that these varying practices were not hostile to Christianity, were not demanded of everyone, and were pursued by Christian individuals for the purposes of their own personal devotional development. In short, Tatian was not prepared to employ Justin's sense that certain actions were "adiaphora." Indeed, he was not prepared to follow the apostle Paul's earlier teaching that, for example, one person might eat meat, while another abstained, provided both did

42. Pedersen, *Tatian the Assyrian*, 146–49.

43. Irenaeus, *Against the Heresies*, 1.28.1.

44. See Matthew 19:12 and 1 Corinthians 7:1–2.

45. See Romans 14:6, 20–21.

so, not to the other's religious detriment, and always "in honor of the Lord, and [in thankfulness] to God."[46]

In other aspects, Tatian's *Address to the Greeks* is different from a number of other second-century Apologies. Tatian repeatedly used the first person singular rather than the more inclusive first person plural. "The emperor," for example, he wrote, "orders *me* to pay taxes. *I* am ready to pay taxes."[47] The first person singular is a rhetorical device; but it also has the sense of stressing the individual over against society, which, in the first place, may be understood as the church and, in the second place, as wider society. In short, Tatian's use of the first personal singular adds weight to the sense that Tatian was both *contra ecclesiam* (against the church) and *contra mundum* (against the world). The traditional accusations levied by Greco-Roman cities against Christians are mentioned, but more in passing than explicitly. Relations with the Jews are not mentioned, unless one counts his questioning who of Moses and Homer was the more ancient, to which an answer in favor of Moses was integral to his argument for the antiquity and so the credibility of Christianity.

Such differences from the thinking of some other Apologists may be explained partly by Tatian's background and partly by the context of his work. For he had been trained in rhetoric. He was a self-confessed one-time attendee at the theater. He knew the names of great philosophers and the salient features of their teachings, albeit possibly only courtesy of the anthologies then assembled for school use. He had been part of cosmopolitan Rome, with its philosophers, rhetoricians, and *literati*. These facts may, in part, account for Tatian's tone and style. When, however, to that is added Tatian's description of the context in which

46. See Romans 14:6.

47. Tatian, *Address*, 4.1. Emphasis added.

he wrote, readers may well be left with the impression that, in his writings, they have chanced upon something akin to a statement, issued but not open to being countermanded, rather than a defense offered by a Christian, surrounded by Christians, on behalf of their shared faith, for wider debate and, hopefully, approval. It comes then as no surprise both that Tatian drew attention to the fact that he was a "philosopher," educated firstly in Greek and subsequently in Christian learning, and that the concluding remarks of his *Address to the Greeks* further state, almost as a challenge that expects no one to counter it successfully, that:

> knowing who God is and what is his creation, I [*sc*. Tatian] offer myself to you, prepared for my doctrines to be examined whilst holding to my way of life in following God with no possibility of denial.[48]

There is a defiance, almost an arrogance here. Tatian's audience, it would appear, may examine Tatian's views, but, whatever its reply, he will neither amend nor deny either his views or his lifestyle. There is little or no sense of Tatian wanting to woo people from their present beliefs to those of Christianity, as, for example, there is in his teacher Justin's writings. There is a certainty that, to all intents and purposes, seems to preclude conversation, the exchange of differing views, the attending carefully to the beliefs of all involved, and the possibility, on his part, of a change of mind. For Tatian's changing his mind seems inconceivable. Above all, there is no sense of the reader's heart being engaging. *Love* of God and *love* of neighbor are not obvious in his *Address*, something that, in ways, tallies with Tatian's conversion, which was essentially an intellectual conversion. He had been persuaded that the Scriptures, when properly

48. Tatian, *Address*, 42.1.

examined, spoke of their own antiquity, and so evidenced the whole truth concerning monotheism, the creation, and humanity's place within it. Once converted, he then became a "herald of the truth,"[49] proclaiming Christianity (a term that he did not use) as an educational discipline, a corrective teaching, a *paideia* (system of education), a philosophy that was not merely superior to any philosophies of the Greeks—to have admitted that Christianity was superior to any Greek philosophy would have been to have admitted that aspects of the truth of Christianity could be found in the various Greek philosophical teachings of the time—but was the true philosophy, the truth, the whole truth, uniquely to be discovered there.

Tatian's sense that the choice between Hellenistic philosophy and Christianity was binary is also evidenced when his thinking is contrasted with Justin's. Justin, in his search for God, had passed through various philosophical schools. Eventually he committed himself to Christianity. Yet, although he did so, he did not then cease wearing a philosopher's cloak. He did not reject all the philosophical teaching that he previously had encountered. Rather he acknowledged that Greek philosophers like Socrates and Heraclitus, who lived and died long before Christ and who were considered by some to be "atheists" even though they had lived "with reason," were "Christians."[50] So, working with the assumptions that Christianity, though continuous with classical Greek *paideia*, had superseded it, Justin recognized that there was certain common ground between Christianity and the Greco-Roman world before which he sought to make his defense. So, he readily entered into discussion with, at least in name, the emperors, whom he titled "philosophers and guardians of justice and lovers of

49. Tatian, *Address*, 17.1.

50. Justin, *Apology*, 1.46.

paideia."[51] In short, Justin worked with the assumption that Christianity was *both continuous with and yet superior to* Hellenistic thinking and teaching. Tatian also worked his way through various philosophical schools. Indeed, at the close of his *Address*, he wrote, "I, Tatian, . . . [was] educated first in [Greek] learning."[52] However, in time, he decided that there was no value in the Greek learning to which previously he had closely attended. He concluded that the teachings of the schools of Greek philosophy were riddled with errors and contradictions, and supportive of nothing but an immoral way of life. Faced therefore with what he saw as a binary choice, that between Greek and Christian learning, he relinquished the "learning in which he had first been educated" and henceforth described himself as "a philosopher amongst the barbarians [*sc.* non-Greek, gentile Christians]," someone now unreservedly committed to this newly chosen "way of life in following God"[53]—in short, a lover of the Christian truth. Unlike Justin, his teacher, Tatian saw *no continuity* between even certain aspects of Hellenistic philosophical thinking and Christianity, even if any such continuity might be deemed to be one qualified by Christianity, which superseded it. Equally, unlike Justin, Tatian also therefore found no common ground for debate and discussion with those brought up in Greek *paideia*, whom he hoped to persuade, if not of the authenticity of Christianity, at least of the impropriety of their criticism of Christians. All that Tatian could do, and indeed did do, therefore was to highlight the errors of Greek learning, and hope that, as the penny had dropped in his case, so it would in the case of those whom he addressed, that they, like him, in the best of all worlds, would forsake entirely Greek learning, Greek

51. Justin, *Apology*, 1.2.

52. Tatian, *Address*, 42.

53. Tatian, *Address*, 42.

paideia, and commit themselves unreservedly to Christianity, the "philosophy amongst the barbarians."

Given such, Tatian's *Address to the Greeks*, with its
hermeneutical method, which did not tolerate other
methodologies, is interesting in its insisting that if only
its readers would be like Tatian, "taught by God,"[54] they
would immediately see the error of their ways and turn to
the one and only truth.

ATHENAGORAS'S *PLEA*

Assuming that Athenagoras's reference to the empire's en-
joying "a deep peace"[55] is not simply a rhetorical flourish,
his *Plea* may be dated to c.176–178, the year 178 being the
year in which war against the Germans resumed. The *Plea*
was addressed to Marcus Aurelius and his son, Commodus, emperors, but "above all, philosophers."[56] That said,
the mention of the emperors, although important for reasons of dating the work, is, in all probability, simply the
result of the text having been written in a forensic style,
in accordance with the then rules of rhetoric. Emperors
of that time, as has already been remarked, did, on occa-
sions, receive embassies, in order to deal with particular
issues affecting a large tranche of their people. The issues
that Athenagoras addressed, namely, the traditional anti-
Christian charges of atheism, involvement in cannibalism,
Thyestean feasts, promiscuous Oedipean intercourse, and
the even more general charge of being called a "Christian," were important issues, but not such as affected a large
tranche of the public. Moreover, since the time of Nero,
long set speeches, which is what, to all intents and purposes,

54. Tatian, *Address*, 29.

55. Athenagoras, *Plea*, 1.2.

56. Athenagoras, *Plea*, 1.1.

the *Plea* is, had given way to point by point investigations. Given such, Athenagoras's likely audience probably was the legal agents of the two emperors mentioned in the opening lines of the *Plea*, and, indirectly, those accused of the traditional anti-Christian charges, who, on reading the *Plea*, might explore possible lines of defense.

The charge of immorality is dealt with, partly by describing the high moral standards by which Christians lived, and partly by stressing that Christianity, unlike the thinking of the various philosophical schools, witnessed to its truth through its power to transform the lives of people of all ages and classes, all of whom took seriously their responsibilities before the Maker and Judge of all people.

It is, however, the charge of atheism that dominates the work. Athenagoras sought to demonstrate that Christians were not atheists. Rather, he maintained, they worshipped the one, true God. So Athenagoras continued the Apologists's redefinition of "atheism." For Athenagoras's one God called into question the truth of the ancient religions that had established the political values of the empire and that emperors long had welcomed as the ungirding of their empire's stability. Indeed, like other Apologists, Athenagoras's understanding of God went further than questioning the traditional cults and the common demands that all peoples should sacrifice to the gods of the empire's temples. It denied the traditional cults. It refused requests to sacrifice in the temples. For it argued that the one God of Christianity only was to be worshipped, a God for whom every believer should be willing to die.

To justify this radical, exclusive theology Athenagoras turned to the best of ancient philosophies; and, by the "best," he meant that which was harmonious with, and so was an "entry point" to, Christianity's deeper insights into the truth. So, for example, he employed against the religions of the time the arguments of Euhemerism, which reasoned that the pagan gods once had been human beings who, in time, were then honored and then further elevated to the status of gods. Pagan gods were "gods" in name alone, but never in nature. Thinking that a philosopher's soul could have been touched by the breath of God and so could have spoken of the truth, Athenagoras drew upon such summaries of philosophy as Doxographies. Yet Athenagoras then went beyond the best of these philosophies. Indeed, he turned to the Hebrew Scriptures, convinced that their prophets were God's musical instruments which sounded forth God's full truth. Their writings, he concluded, were the ancient expressions of the faith taught by Christians, and the antiquity of their writings was evidence that Christianity was not a "new" religion, wanting in not having an ancient heritage.

Athenagoras was not therefore one who argued *contra mundum*. He recognized good in imperial and civic life. Indeed, he expressed loyalty to the emperors and gratitude for the imperial peace, which he believed made for a tranquil life even for Christians. He recognized a degree of harmony between the best of ancient philosophies and Christianity. So, he was ready to use philosophy as an aid to his audience's apprehending Christian truth, and as a basis for pleading for the state to act ever more reasonably, not simply by its no longer making false charges against Christians, but by its citizens becoming Christians, because Christians both were the true theists and were, above all, concerned for the empire's wellbeing, truly realized in and through the one, true God. For Athenagoras, Christianity was not just another force for good, but *the* force for the empire's good.

THEOPHILOS OF ANTIOCH

Theophilos was the bishop of Antioch [c.170–early 180s], a city then and still in John Chysostom's time [c.380–390] strongly influenced by Hellenistic Judaism.[57] He wrote his *Letter to Autolycus*, a pagan, in c.180.[58] Theophilos's letter breathes the atmosphere of the city in which it was written. Although Christian in tone and missionary in purpose, it reflects the late Jewish apologetic of the Hellenistic synagogue. It dismisses Greek philosophy generally as contradictory, even as it dismisses Plato in particular as self-contradictory. Only insofar as Greek philosophers had stolen from the Hebrew prophets did they reflect the truth. Certainly philosophy was not for Theophilos as it was for Clement of Alexandria [fl.180–203], "a teacher to bring [Hellenists] to Christ."[59] Having then dismissed Greek philosophy, Theophilos resorted mainly to a Jewish legacy. He frequently quoted from the Hellenistic-Jewish Sibylline Oracles. He referred to Josephus's apologetic treatise, *Against Apion*. He titled Moses as "our prophet," who delivered "the law to the whole world, although especially to the Jews."[60] Even though he understood God's Word as the innate Word of God (the Word *endiathetos*), who is then uttered (the Word *prophorikos*) in order to create, an understanding developed in the light of Stoic thinking, even here Theophilos was much reliant on the

57. John Chrysostom, *Against the Jews*, PG 48. 844.

58. Theophilos's Roman chronology ends with the death of the emperor Verus, co-regent with Marcus Aurelius. Verus died in 169, having reigned, according to Theophilos, for nineteen years. In all probability Theophilos has here made a mistake, and had intended to refer to Marcus Aurelius's death in March 180, he having reigned for nineteen years, from 161–180.

59. Clement of Alexandria, *Miscellanies*, 1.5.28.

60. Theophilos, *To Autolycus*, 3.9; 18 and 23.

Hellenistic-Jewish understanding of God's Word as it is reflected in the thinking of, amongst others, Philo.[61]

Given such, Theophilos understood the immorality of the pagan gods as evidence that these gods were not gods. He dismissed pagan practices as those that introduced and established impiety in individual lives. So, unable to look to Greek philosophy or literature for guidance, and despairing of the pagan way of life, he turned to the Hebrew Scriptures, and especially Moses and the prophets, for more ancient, and what he therefore saw as much more reliable, sources for his strictly monotheistic theology and his exacting Christian ethics. These Hebrew Scriptures he then read in an essentially Jewish way, understanding them primarily in a literal manner. So, in the main, he understood, for example, the creation narrative in Genesis. When he did venture beyond understanding a text literally, he generally understood it as prefiguring Christian beliefs, as is the case when he found hints in the Hebrew Scriptures to the Christian doctrines of baptism and of the future resurrection.[62] Alongside this strong Jewish heritage, it would seem from allusions and quotations that Theophilos also was reliant upon at least three Gospels—Matthew, Luke, and John—and upon the Pauline corpus, including the Pastoral Epistles. That said, he mentions neither Jesus nor Paul.

Perhaps Theophilos's choice of authoritative sources is understandable. For he was tailoring his writing to the inhabitants of a city still strongly influenced by Hellenistic Judaism, and in doing that, maybe he was not so different from the other mid-to-late second-century Apologists who also framed their writings in the language and thought of their particular and immediate readership.

61. Philo, *On Flight*, 95.
62. E.g., Theophilos, *To Autolycus*, 2.16 and 2.14.

QUESTIONS FOR REFLECTION
AND DISCUSSION

1. The writing of many of the early Apologists sought to lead their readers not only to know *about* the God of the Christians, but also to *know* that self-same God. Theologically speaking, is there a place for Christian apologetics being limited to introducing people solely to knowing about God?

2. Some of the Apologists spoke of their having been "taught by God" through people who were "musical instruments" played by God. What consequences do such have for those who would learn of God but are less persuaded of such immediacy of God's manner of teaching?

3. If an individual chances upon a particular religion that encompasses what Aristides called "the truth concerning God," is it sufficient that that person gives it mental assent? If not, what more is required?

4. Are there such people as "Christians before Christ"? If there are, what may profitably be learned from them?

5. The Apologists were divided in their answers to the question of the value, or otherwise, of non-Christian philosophical reflection to their seeking to understand Christian faith. What criteria should be used now when faced with the same question?

3

CHRISTIANITY—NOT NEW, AND IT IS TRUE

THE MID-TO-LATE SECOND-CENTURY APOLOGISTS were adamant that Christianity was *not new* and was *true*. Theophilos, for example, stressed that Christian teaching was "neither modern nor mere fables";[1] Tatian robustly countered charges that his Christian beliefs were "new-fangled barbarian doctrines";[2] and Justin, though not listing novelty as one of the charges brought against Christianity, denied that what he and other Christians confessed with regards to Christ were "mere marvelous tales."[3] Indeed, employing themes common to the Apologists's general defense of Christianity's antiquity, he asked,

> Why should we believe . . . that [a crucified man] is the firstborn of the unbegotten God and will

1. Theophilos, *To Autolycus*, 3.16.

2. Tatian, *Address*, 35.2.

3. Justin, *Apology*, 1.54.

> pass judgement on the entire human race unless
> we have found testimony concerning him made
> public before he came and was born as man.[4]

Severally, and together, the Apologists either asserted or assumed that Christianity both was not new and was true; and this they asserted within a Greco-Roman world where, generally speaking, a belief's antiquity sustained its claim to be true, even as a belief's novelty undermined its truth claim.[5]

The arguments of the Apologists that Christianity was not novel but antique are several and widely shared: the Hebrew prophets, amongst whom Moses was placed, were, in the words of Justin, "our teachers,"[6] teachers from whom Christians had received instruction concerning creation itself,[7] Christ and the gentile mission,[8] and the final

---

4. Justin, *Apology*, 1.53.

5. The contrasting of what is "new" with what is old, traditional, and venerable—to the detriment, if not the total undermining of the former—is a common strategy used by critics of Christianity, and by Christians against some teachers and groups whose claim to be Christian was considered suspect. See Suetonius, *Lives of the Caesars*, 5.16, which refers to Christianity as a "new religion" [*superstitio nova ac malefacta*], a cult without the redeeming virtues of the old religions; Irenaeus, *Against the Heresies*, 3.4.1–2. See also Irenaeus, *Against the Heresies*, 3.3.2, where the "tradition of the truth" maintained by the church is contrasted with the "inventions [*sc.* that which is new] of the heretics"; and those fourth-century theologians who were one in their condemnation of the various forms of Arianism, but, in answering the question of how the Son's full divinity was related to that of God the Father, adamantly denied the creative novelty of their own views, claiming that their particular positions were at least implicit in the earlier traditions of the church.

6. Justin, *Apology*, 1.59.

7. Theophilos, *To Autolycus*, 3.23.

8. Justin, *Apology*, 1.31.

judgement.[9] Indeed, Christianity's antiquity, the Apologists argued, was underlined by the extraordinary antiquity of Moses, the first prophet: Moses, they maintained, antedated Homer, the "oldest of poets and historians."[10] He antedated the Trojan war, of which Homer wrote, by either four hundred[11] or one thousand years.[12] Indeed, they asserted, he antedated the ancient cities of Egypt.[13] It is not surprising then that both Justin and Theophilos claimed that Moses was more ancient than all the Greek writers and poets.[14] Comparatively speaking, they then implied, it was Greco-Roman thinking, rather than Christianity, which was novel, and whose truths claims were suspect.

Within this context, Athenagoras's silence concerning Moses's remote antiquity may therefore seem a strange silence. Perhaps, however, his silence, though noticeable, is not total. Certainly, in mentioning the charges levelled against Christians, Athenagoras recorded those of atheism, Thyestean feasts, and Oedipean unions,[15] but not that of Christianity's novelty. Elsewhere, however, he did state the grounds for Christian believing:

> we [*sc.* Christians] have prophets as witnesses
> to what we think and believe, witnesses driven
> by a divinely inspired Spirit to speak about God
> and the things of God. . . . It would therefore be
> irrational, he continued, to abandon belief in the
> Spirit from God who has moved the prophets's

9. Theophilos. *To Autolycus*, 2.10. See also Justin, *Apology*, 1.52.

10. Tatian, *Plea*, 31.1.

11. Tatian, *Plea*, 39.1.

12. Theophilos, *To Autolycus*, 3.20.

13. Theophilos, *To Autolycus*, 3.20.

14. Justin, *Apology*, 1.44; 1.54; Theophilos, *To Autolycus*, 2.30; 2.33.

15. Athenagoras, *Plea*, 3.1.

> mouths like musical instruments and to attend
> to human opinions.[16]

These "prophets" were not named here by Athenagoras. Yet, it would be strange not to identify amongst them Moses, Isaiah, and Jeremiah, prophets to whom Athenagoras more generally referred in his writings, and to whom other Apologists referred when seeking to refute the charge of Christianity being novel. Further, Athenagoras's reference here to the godly inspiration of these prophets's utterances echoes the thinking of other Apologists when they treated the charge that Christianity was but a recent human invention. Athenagoras's thinking in these matters may therefore be not so dissimilar from that of other contemporary and near contemporary Apologists.

The Apologists indeed reinforced their argument that the Hebrew prophets—who, they claimed, foretold the truths later held by Christians—were more ancient than the Greek poets and philosophers by maintaining that these latter were dependent for some of their ideas upon the beliefs of these former. Plato, they asserted, "borrowed" from Moses:[17] he depended upon Moses for his views on God's creation of the world,[18] the soul's immortality, *postmortem* punishment, and the contemplation of things heavenly.[19] They even maintained that the Greek poets and philosophers had "stolen" from the law and the prophets of the Hebrew Scriptures such beliefs as the world's conflagration, the connection between righteousness, judgement, and punishment, the divine providential care of the

---

16. Athenagoras, *Plea*, 7.3.

17. Justin, *Apology*, 1.44.

18. Justin, *Apology*, 1.59.

19. Justin, *Apology*, 1.44.

living and the dead, and God's oneness.[20] If Plato and his fellow philosophers and the poets were from of old, and if they had borrowed or even "stolen" ideas from Moses and his fellow prophets, then Moses and his fellow prophets, the Apologists argued, manifestly were from a yet more ancient time. Thus, Christianity, which learned its truths from the prophets of the Hebrew Scriptures, clearly was not novel, but venerable.

The Apologists also found evidence for Christianity's antiquity in the Christ being, in both word and deed, the fulfilment of that foretold by the prophets.[21] The incarnation, an Apologist such a Justin admitted, may have been a relatively recent event. Indeed, Justin readily referred to the birth of Jesus "in a village in the land of the Jews, thirty five stadia from Jerusalem, . . . as you [*sc.* the emperors] can also ascertain from the registers of taxation levied under Cyrenius, your first procurator in Judaea."[22] He pointed to the possibility that the emperors could learn of Jesus's miracles "from the acts of Pontius Pilate."[23] He spoke of Jesus's crucifixion "under Pontius Pilate, procurator of Judaea, in the time of Tiberius Caesar"[24] "in Judaea, . . . after whose crucifixion the land was straightway surrendered to [the emperors] as the spoil of war."[25] Christianity, in that sense at least, Justin allowed, was "new." It was, however, at one and the same time, also as old as could be. For the one recently born was the one who also was older than the world. For, as Justin also maintained, there was a "oneness" in him who

20. Theophilos, *To Autolycus*, 2.38. See also Tatian, *Plea*, 29.2.

21. See Justin, *Apology* 1.12; 1.30–37; Theophilos, *To Autolycus*, 2.10.

22. Justin, *Apology*, 1.34.

23. Justin, *Apology*, 1.48.

24. Justin, *Apology*, 1.13.

25. Justin, *Apology*, 1.32.

made the world, who spoke through the prophets, who became human in fulfilment of the prophets's foretelling, and who would return to judge both the living and the dead. So, Justin concluded, those who alleged that Christianity was new because Jesus only recently had lived on this earth had failed to appreciate that the God who was active in and through that Jesus had been active in the world for as long as the world had existed and would exist; and it was of this Christ that Christianity spoke.

Making the same point, but in a different manner, Justin and Theophilos maintained that Moses was "*our* prophet," the prophets of the Hebrew Scriptures were "*our* teachers," the Hebrew Scriptures were "*our* Scriptures," and the people of Israel were "*our* ancestors."[26] The Hebrew prophets and their prophecies were not long gone people and distant words who and which, once upon a time, had pointed to the now recent Word incarnate and his present followers, the Christians, but were the Christians's prophets, "our" prophets. Their Scriptures were "our" Scriptures, telling of "our" fulfilment in "our" Christ. It was true that the incarnation, a relatively recent occurrence, was to be recognized as a climax. Yet, for Apologists like Justin and Theophilos, that was not the whole truth. For, for them, the incarnation was also the natural culmination of that far more extended process of God's self-unveiling, an unveiling already encountered in the words of the prophets of the Hebrew Scriptures. At one and the same time the incarnation therefore was both a climax and the end of a process. So, what was new was also, in truth, also *very ancient*.

It was, the Apologists then argued, using a trope of the times, that very venerable antiquity that helped to evidence Christianity's credibility. Theophilos and Tatian particularly

26. Justin, *Apology*, 1.59; Theophilos, *To Autolycus*, 3.18; 2.30; 3.26; 3.20 respectively. The italics are mine.

employed this argument. The former brought his *Letter to Autolycus* to an end by writing "one can see the antiquity of the prophetic writing and the divinity of our doctrine, and that therefore [our] doctrine is not recent nor are our tenets mythical and false . . . but very ancient and true."[27] Tatian, who converted to Christianity in part because he was convinced that the Hebrew Scriptures were older than the writings of the Greeks,[28] meanwhile argued that the seeker after truth, even as Tatian himself had been, "should believe [Moses] who was prior in time, in preference to the Greeks who learned their doctrines at second hand."[29]

More theological arguments, in favor of the thesis that Christianity was true, ensue. For, while Christianity's venerable antiquity might have evidenced its truth, it was the Spirit of God who guaranteed its truth. For it was this prophetic Spirit who inspired the prophets,[30] so completely inspiring them that Athenagoras was content to liken the Spirit's using the prophets to deliver God's message to a flautist using a flute to deliver his music.[31] For Athenagoras then there was an immediacy between the Spirit of truth and the veracity of the words of the prophets. Theophilos also was happy to refer to the Hebrew prophets as "God's instruments."[32] Using another image, he described them as "God-taught."[33] It followed, the Apologists therefore argued, that Christians, relying on the ancient prophets, did indeed speak and live

27. Theophilos, *To Autolycus*, 3.29.

28. Tatian, *Plea*, 29.1.

29. Tatian, *Plea*, 40.1.

30. Justin, *Apology*, 1.31; 1.59. See also Justin, *Apology*, 1.36, where it is the divine Word who inspired the prophets; Athenagoras, *Plea*, 7.3; 9.3; Theophilos, *To Autolycus*, 2.11; 2.30.

31. Athenagoras, *Plea*, 9.1. See also Athenagoras, *Plea*, 7.3.

32. Theophilos, *To Autolycus*, 2.10.

33. Athenagoras, *Plea*, 11.1; Theophilos, *To Autolycus*, 2.10.

and teach the God-taught truth. As Athenagoras asserted, Christians said "nothing unsupported by evidence, . . . but are exponents of what the prophets uttered."[34]

Like the "God-taught" prophets of old, Christians now also were the "God-taught."[35] Indeed, that Christians were "God taught" and not merely worldly wise was evidenced, the Apologists argued, in the fact that Christians generally were simple, humble people. They were, according to Tatian, people whose words lacked arrogance and whose speech was artless.[36] As the prophets were "illiterates and shepherds and uneducated"[37]—allusions to Moses, who claimed not to be eloquent,[38] to David, the former shepherd, and to Jeremiah, who asserted that he did not know how to speak[39]—so Christians, who had learned from these prophets, were those who did "not know even the shape of letters, who [were] uneducated and barbarous in speech."[40] What they taught therefore manifestly did not originate in them. Rather, it originated in God, and became theirs in and through the "God taught" prophets of the ancient Hebrew Scriptures. Humble before God, not "bigoted in their opinions, nor . . . governed by their passions,"[41] Christians therefore stood in marked contrast with the Greek poets and philosophers. For these latter, being unwilling to humble themselves to learn about God from God himself,[42] had relied upon their own creaturely conjectures and

34. Athenagoras, *Plea*, 24.5.

35. Theophilos, *To Autolycus*, 2.33.

36. Tatian, *Address*, 29.2.

37. Theophilos, *To Autolycus*, 2.35.

38. Exodus 4:10–11.

39. See Jeremiah 1:6.

40. Justin, *Apology*, 1.60.

41. Justin, *Apology*, 1.53.

42. Athenagoras, *Plea*, 7.2.

conceptions.[43] These misconceptions, Theophilos maintained, they then had wrapped in a human eloquence, so giving these misconceptions verisimilitude. It was therefore important, Theophilos asserted, that those who attended poetry readings and plays or who were minded to listen to the teachings of philosophers were mindful of the untruths embedded, but artfully disguised, in their poems and teachings.[44] So, the Apologists argued, it was not just better but essential that anyone desiring to discern and then to live according to the truth should turn from what Tatian bluntly described as the many doctrines incoherently based in "Roman arrogance and Athenian cold cleverness"[45] and turn to the Spirit-filled, God-taught Christians.

Behind this contrast of the humble and often illiterate Christian, dependent on God's self-revelation, with the arrogant Greek, not all of whose glittering, eloquent teaching was gold, lie a number of significant themes. Firstly, many Hellenistic philosophers of the time still propounded Plato's teaching that, "to discover the Maker and Father of this universe [was] . . . a hard task,"[46] hard indeed, *but humanly achievable.* Christians, meanwhile, held that it was those whose hearts had been made pure who would see God,[47] something achievable only insofar as people so humbled themselves that they placed themselves in a state of readiness to receive divine revelation. For Christianity, therefore, any knowledge of the Creator and Father of all, even if mediated through the prophets of old, ultimately was from God alone. All such knowledge was a *gift*, never earned. It was ever graciously offered and always open to being thankfully

43. Theophilos, *To Autolycus*, 2.8. See also. Athenagoras, *Plea*, 7.2.

44. Theophilos, *To Autolycus*, 2.12.

45. See Tatian, *Address*, 35.1.

46. Plato, *Timaeus* 28C.

47. So Matthew 5:8.

received. For the Apologists, therefore, God is the active one
and humans are the passive ones, "passive" in the sense that,
if they would know the truth, they needed—*capax Dei* (capable of receiving God) though they had been made—to lay
themselves before the gracious God and in humble patience
await God's self-disclosure. In contrast with the thinking
of many of the Hellenistic philosophers then, the emphasis
here lay on *God's initiative*. Anything therefore born of conjecture, for the Christians, was then but a human invention,
an erroneous conception, or, as Tatian might has said, an
"idol," a work of human minds.

In contrast with the thinking of the early fourth century, when, in terms of a doctrine of creation, the ontologi-
cal distinction generally had moved from that between the
material and the spiritual to that between the created—into
which category the human soul and mind were placed—
and the Creator,[48] the role of the human in discerning God,
as envisaged by the Apologists, may seem to have been
thought to have been substantial. For, to the Apologists,
the human soul was deemed to have had a certain kinship,
albeit a created kinship, with its divine Maker; and so, when
individuals purified that kinship, their knowledge of God
was increasingly realized. In that sense, a human being had
to work at knowing God.

Yet, in comparison with the thinking of late second-
century philosophy, the role of the human in discerning
God, as envisaged by the Apologists, seems to have been
much less substantial. For, in the view of the Apologists,
people, though needing to work at knowing God, were to
work at knowing God by humbling themselves, opening
themselves to God in and through allowing their hearts to
be made pure, and accepting that divine self-revelation. In
contrast with pagan philosophy of the time, the Apologists's

48. Louth, *The Origins of the Christian Mystical Tradition*, 75–77.

thinking held that people desirous to know God were to be "passive" in the sense of becoming "receptive" to God's gracious initiative. Any "work" involved in the process of learning of God and discerning God was therefore less an active "doing" and more a *subduing oneself that one might receive God's gift*. Expressed pictorially, people were to allow themselves to be the flutes,[49] which they have been made to be, to be played by the Spirit of God. As a flute was to be "passive" in the hands of a flautist, waiting to give expression to a flautist's composition, so individuals were to be instruments in the hands of the Spirit, open to expressing the Spirit of God's truths. For the Apologists, therefore, it was not that people had no role whatsoever in learning and sharing the truths of God. Rather, it was that they had an important, but *subsidiary* role, one that honored God's primacy in all things.

Secondly, on account of the subtle, eloquent beauty with which the Greek poets and philosophers clothed their words, their utterances, the Apologists reflected, often *appeared* trustworthy and true. In contrast, the utterances of the ancient but artless prophets and of the later simple Christians, the Apologists further reflected, often *appeared* foolish. Appearances, however, often are deceptive, and so, the Apologists held, they were in these cases. The words of the ancient prophets and the then Christians might well have been prosaic and unembellished. Yet, at one and the same time as being the words on the lips of mere mortals, these words were also, the Apologists maintained, words derived from the Spirit of God, the Spirit of Truth. They were *human words bearing divine truth* and so were trustworthy and true. In contrast, the words of the poets and philosophers were but human words, vehicles bearing mere human

49. See Athenagoras, *Plea*, 9.1 and Athenagoras, *Plea*, 7.3.

opinions, no more trustworthy than the fickle minds of the fallible people who framed them.

Thirdly, and closely related to the previous point, is the matter of *evangelism*. The Greek poets and philosophers were, the Apologists suggested, possessed of human thoughts that, relying on eloquent packaging, they sought to sell. Their eloquence, the Apologists however posited, did not help in the process of "selling." For, in truth, it generally but drew attention to the Greek orators and, by drawing attention to the orators, signaled to those who had minds to discern, that what the orators essentially expressed was but the product of their mere human minds. The prophets of the Hebrew Scriptures and the Christians, in contrast, proffered divine treasures, which "sold" themselves. These divine treasures may often have been packaged ineloquently. Yet, curiously, that very fact actually helped in the "selling." For the speaker's very inarticulateness turned the hearer's attention from the speaker to the divine Being of whom they spoke. Like earthen vessels containing treasure,[50] the very ordinariness of the words of the prophets and Christians highlighted the great and extraordinary worth of the One of whom they spoke. Like the carpenter of Nazareth, whose ordinariness, as even his contemporaries realized, highlighted the wisdom and the authority with which he spoke,[51] so the Christians—many of whom were but children or women, whom their contemporaries commonly viewed as immature or feeble and unreliable—through their very ordinariness drew attention to the wonderful and extraordinary truth upon their lips. Indeed, there is a sense in which, like the prophets, whose inglorious frailty, rather than hindering others as they sought after God, drew the attention of others to the

50. See 2 Corinthians 4:7.

51. See Mark 6:2–3 and Matthew 13:54–56.

glory of God, Christians, ordinary, everyday people, did not prove an obstruction to their contemporaries who were seeking divine truth but rather highlighted for them the extraordinary glory of God. So, Justin argued, extraordinary, divine insights, in being shared by very ordinary humans, might the more readily convince their hearers to "understand that these [insights] are not the result of human wisdom, but are uttered by God's power."[52] The truth of God, Justin implied, was therefore not only graciously given but also graciously shared. For it was shared in such a way as to hinder a person from lauding those who are "God taught" rather than God. It was expressed in not so sophisticated a manner as to be incomprehensible to the average person. It was delivered in not so pressing a style as to overwhelm a person's freedom to believe. Justin's thinking here is therefore not dissimilar from Diognetus's unnamed correspondent's when the latter explained that God came as an infant, not to force belief, but to persuade, compulsion not being "God's way of working."[53]

Two further arguments for the truth of Christianity were marshalled by the Apologists. The first argument was centered upon Christianity's singleness of message, and the second upon the fulfilment of prophecies. Theophilos especially propounded the first. The prophets, he observed, were many and had lived over a very long period of time. Yet, for all that, each, he asserted, had "spoken things constant and harmonious one with another,"[54] a unanimity evidencing that every prophet, in each's own particular times, had been "given utterances by the one and same Spirit,"[55] the Source and Guarantor of all truth. In contrast,

52. Justin, *Apology*, 1.60.
53. *To Diognetus*, 7.4.
54. Theophilos, *To Autolycus*, 2.10; 2.11; 2.35; 3.17.
55. Theophilos, *To Autolycus*, 2.35; 3.17.

Greek philosophy, apart from those aspects in which it was consistent with Christianity, was judged by people such as Justin as being "many-headed."[56] In many ways and places it was held to be contradictory.[57] So, insofar as it was such, the Apologists concluded that it either had not originated from the One God, or, if it had once so originated, it had since been corrupted,[58] often splintering, and sometimes becoming so fractured that, as writers such as Athenagoras were ready to maintain, Greek religions were reduced to but man-made myths in which the gods were morally no better, and often far worse than mere mortals.[59] So, the Apologists concluded, pagan philosophies, insofar as they were inconsistent, were not true. For truth, by its very nature, was deemed always to be simple. Nor were they trustworthy, in that, being internally discordant, they not only undermined each other[60] but also potentially confused, if not hindered, anyone seeking after the one, consistent, harmonious, and only true God.

The second argument for Christianity's truth relied upon a prophecy's fulfilment. In his *First Apology* Justin reflected upon what he saw as the fulfilment of Hebrew prophecies concerning the incarnation. These prophetic fulfillments he then read to be evidence that, as Christianity rightly taught, not only was the world ruled, not by chance, but by God's providence—for "to tell of a thing before it happens and then to show it happening as it was foretold" is God's work[61]—but also the Jesus of the Christians truly was

56. Justin, *Dialogue with Trypho*, 2.

57. Athenagoras, *Plea*, 7.2; Theophilos, *To Autolycus*, 2.5; Tatian, *Address*, 25.1–2.

58. See Theophilos, *To Autolycus*, 2.12.

59. Athenagoras, *Plea*, 10.2.

60. Theophilos, *To Autolycus*, 3.3; 3.7–8.

61. Justin, *Apology*, 1.12.

the Son of God. "With our own eyes," Justin confidently asserted, "we see things that have, and are happening, just as
they were predicted. This, we think, will appear even to you
[*sc.* the emperors] as the strongest and truest evidence."[62]
Indeed, some Apologists argued, fulfilled prophecies properly were to be seen to be the grounds for taking seriously
not only what the prophets once prophesied about Christ
but also what they said, firstly, about the time from the
world's creation to the Apologists's own time and, secondly,
about the end-time. So, for example, Theophilos argued,
since the prophets had been proven to be trustworthy in
what they had said about the Christ, they ought also now
to be trusted in what they had said "about the epochs and
eras before [*sc.* Noah's] flood."[63] Extending this argument,
the Apologists then further maintained that, as the ancient
prophets had been proven right in their predictions of what
had already occurred, they would further be proven right
in their predictions of what was yet to come to pass. For
that reason, Justin and Theophilos asserted, the prophets
and their utterances were to be heeded.[64] Here again the
Apologists sought to establish the case for the ancient and
venerable truth of Christianity.

Such were the main responses by the Apologists to the
charges, explicit and implicit, that Christianity was novel,
a recent concoction of mere fables. These responses, however, were not their only responses. For, as generally is be
recognized, the Apologists saw their task as being not only
the refutation of what they deemed to be false accusations
but also the persuasion of any who would listen to their
apologetics to turn from their present, mistaken beliefs to
the venerable truths of Christianity itself.

62. Justin, *Apology*, 1.30; 1.33; 1.53.
63. Theophilos, *To Autolycus*, 3.17. See also *To Autolycus*, 2.10.
64. Justin, *Apology*, 1.52. See also Theophilos, *To Autolycus*, 2.10.

As mentioned earlier, the Apologists maintained that the Greek poets and philosophers had borrowed, or even stolen, from the Hebrew Scriptures their belief in God's one-ness and, consequent on that belief in God's oneness, their beliefs in the world's origin, the providential care of all that exists, and the fiery end of everything. Given this mention of borrowing, it is then notable that the Apologists did not *criticize* the Greeks for borrowing, let alone condemn them for failing to acknowledge their having borrowed what Justin understood to be "seeds of truth."[65] Rather, the Apologists saw there an apologetic opportunity. For they did not believe—as is evidenced in Theophilos's reflection that the Egyptian and Chaldean prophets should have been able to tell accurately of the devastating flood of Noah's time, had they but allowed themselves to be led by the pure, divine Spirit[66]—that God had elected to reveal himself to only the Hebrew prophets, whose writing were, in turn, available to only those who subsequently became Christians.

For the Apologists certain corollaries followed from the recognition both that the Greeks "borrowed" certain truths, originally revealed by God through the Hebrew prophets, and that God's truth was intended for all. That there had been such borrowing added to the argument that the truths held by Christians were more ancient than any ideas held by the Greek poets and philosophers. It estab-lished that the views of the Greek poets and philosophers were not "equal" to those of the Christians. As Justin was eager to stress, "it is not that we [Christians] hold the same views as others [such as Plato], but that all speak in imitation of us."[67] The Greeks might have taught aspects of the truth; but they had not taught the whole truth. Their

65. Justin, *Apology*, 1.44.

66. Theophilos, *To Autolycus*, 2.33.

67. Justin, *Apology*, 1.60.

views were therefore to be judged in the light of God's self-revelation, known through the Hebrew prophets and in and through the Christ, and then only to be counted as authoritative inasmuch as they were one with the faith of Christians. Further, and more positively, the assertions that the Greeks had borrowed certain truths from the Hebrew Scriptures and that the truths revealed in and through the self-same Scriptures were not to be the "property" of only one particular group of people, but were to be owned by all, meant that, insofar as Hellenistic views were consonant with Christianity, Hellenistic views might, and should, be the basis for dialogue, the means whereby a conversation might take place, which could lead to the conversion of Greeks to Christianity.

Examples of such conversations include those of Justin with Greek philosophers as he affirmed Plato's reflections on human culpability[68] and questioned Plato's positing that God's Son was placed cross-wise in the universe.[69] In this latter case, Justin maintained that Plato's idea was mistaken, the result of a misreading of Numbers 21:6–9, the correct reading of which should have led Plato to posit "a figure of the cross." Wise disciples of Plato who were open to learning from such a corrective conversation were therefore encouraged to revisit the book of Numbers, which Justin attributed to Moses, one of Justin's Hebrew prophets, to read it as their master Plato had done, but to conclude other than as their master had done. Rereading the passage aright, they would then see there a sign or symbol of the cross whence came salvation and life in abundance for the whole universe.

Interestingly, in many ways, this borrowing by Greeks from the writings of Moses and the other Hebrew prophets

68. Justin, *Apology*, 1.44.

69. Justin, *Apology*, 1.60. See also Plato, *Timaeus* 8.36B–C.

was seen as not dissimilar from what the Christians had done when they made Moses *their* prophet and the Hebrew Scriptures *their* Scriptures. For Christians had, in a sense, "borrowed" from the Hebrew prophets. The main differences then between Greek and Christian "borrowing" were that the Greeks had not recognized, let alone admitted, both that, in certain instances, they had borrowed "seeds of truth" from the Hebrew prophets, and that what they had borrowed they had then often corrupted. Christians, in contrast, had recognized and acknowledged their dependency upon Moses and others, and had been accurate and faithful in their borrowing. That said, when any borrowing was honest and accurate, those who borrowed—in the case of the Greeks, in part, and in that of Christians, in full— were thereby showing, even if not always acknowledging, their common dependency upon God and God's chosen manner of self-disclosure.

What, to the thinking of the Apologists, was, however, particularly problematic was inaccurate borrowing, or an unwillingness to borrow at all. Practitioners of the former included both the Jews[70] and Greek philosophers,[71] while those of the latter were those who limited themselves to human conjecture, and so created "gods." As the writer to Diognetus reflected, in language drawn from the Psalter, some created for themselves "gods" in the form of statues, which had mouths "which could not speak" and eyes "which could not see."[72] Athenagoras similarly reflected on poets who created their own myths in which the "gods" were no better than immoral human beings,[73] gods that,

---

70. Justin, *Apology*, 1.36.

71. Justin, *Apology*, 1.44 and 1.60, where Plato especially is mentioned. See also Tatian, *Address*, 29.2

72. *To Diognetus* 2. See also Psalm 115:4–8 and Psalm 135:15–18.

73. Athenagoras, *Plea*, 10.2.

not dissimilar from those of the Psalmist's, also had eyes but could not see the errors of their ways. The issue here for the Apologists was that such gods could not be gods, not primarily because of their inability to speak and see, nor because of their wanting inerrancy and their modelling the very antithesis of virtuous living, but because the one who was true God was *not made by any*, but, being the Maker of all, was uncreated. Hence the gods composed or made by the poets and imagined by the philosophers not being gods; hence the proper human dependency upon God; hence the need to borrow from those to whom God had already revealed himself. Further, these philosophers and poets who did not borrow at all from the Spirit-filled Hebrew prophets, who "made" every aspect of their "gods," often compounded their error of making gods in their own image and likeness by then wrapping these gods in alluring packaging. As Tatian pointedly reflected,

> with much labor the [Greek] sophists tried to counterfeit all that they knew from Moses's teaching . . . in order that, by concealing their ignorance with a cloak of empty words, they might distort the truth as myth;[74]

and, as Theophilos earlier had observed, these myths were clothed with "an *appearance* of trustworthiness."[75] As the apostle Paul's "angel of light"[76] sought to deceive, so these visually attractive statues and verbally persuasive myths sought to deceive, disguising the fact that the opinions that lay behind their making were but empty human opinions, whose vacuity was all the more obvious when set alongside the divine wisdom, received and uttered in former times

74. Tatian, *Address*, 40.1.

75. Theophilos, *To Autolycus*, 2.12. The italics are mine.

76. 2 Corinthians 11:13–15.

by Hebrew prophets.[77] So, poets and philosophers and their audiences were trapped in false cults.

Interestingly, the culpability for this entrapment was not limited to the statues and myths and their makers. It was also laid at the feet of *demons*. Polemics may lie behind such attribution; but so too did a binary theology that saw truth and goodness originating in God, and error and immorality stemming from demons, which, it was here maintained, inspired and encouraged those in their power to speak "at the instance [sc. of the demons] whatever [sc. the demons] said."[78] The criticism implicit in these references is all the more damning when seen alongside the same Apologists's reference to the Hebrew prophets uttering, at God's prompting, whatever God said.[79]

Again and again, a contrast is evident. The Hebrew prophets received *God's* wisdom, while the Greeks invented a *human* "wisdom." That received from the one true God was harmonious, while that conjectured by the Greeks was discordant and contradictory. True divine wisdom was cloaked in human words, in order to accommodate divine wisdom to humanity's frail capacity to recognize and to receive the life-giving wisdom, while mere human "wisdom" was wrapped in seemingly "divine" forms, to seduce people into believing in a counterfeit wisdom that, in turn, led to trust in the opinions of mere mortals. Lastly, while what was spoken through the Hebrew prophets and the Christ sought to lead creation into the paths of righteousness, the various Greek myths were "uttered under the influence of wicked demons, to deceive and to lead the human race astray."[80]

77. Theophilos, *To Autolycus*, 2,10–11.

78. Theophilos, *To Autolycus*, 2.8. see also Justin, *Apology*, 1.54.

79. Theophilos, *To Autolycus*, 2.10–11.

80. Justin, *Apology*, 1.54.

Significantly, that there could be such demonically inspired inaccuracies and, at times, dishonest borrowing from the Hebrew prophets was deemed to be all the worse for two reasons. Firstly, at times Greek philosophers did speak in harmony with the prophets. There was therefore no inevitability that any borrowing would be inaccurate and dishonest. Secondly, what was at stake here was not simply theological opinion but an individual's relationship with the one and only God, whom to serve was to lay oneself open to life everlasting and whom to resist was to risk eternal punishment; and neither an individual's life nor the mercy and justice of God were to be treated lightly.

Given such, the Apologists's responses to the charges that Christianity was new and not true were not simply to argue that it was antique, venerable, and accurate, but also to seek to persuade their audience to turn from their errors and to turn to Christianity, in and through whose God salvation was to be found. It was the Apologists's responsibility then to encourage people to learn and then to live the ancient truth of Christianity, to understand the Word of God as the touchstone by which all the past, from the world's creation, through the times of the Hebrew Scriptures, to the thinking of Greek poets and philosophers were to be judged, to believe in the Christ, the Lord and Master of all godly belief and practice, and to prepare for the Christ's second advent, when God, the judge of all, would mete out to the righteous life everlasting and to the unrighteous unending punishment. It is not without significance, therefore, that Apologists such as Justin, Theophilos, and Tatian each describe their particular conversions from Greek philosophy to Christianity,[81] thereby indirectly inviting others to join them in faithfully following God. Nor is it unimportant

81. See Justin, *Dialogue with Trypho*, 2–8; Theophilos, *To Autolycus*, 1.14; Tatian, *Address* 29–30.

that the author of the *Letter to Diognetus* described the life of Christians as morally compelling and advocated the overflowing joy that is anyone's who will imitate God, who is good and the source of all goodness.[82] For the *Letter to Diognetus* is not simply description; it is testimony seeking the reader's conversion.

In short, for these late second-century Apologists there are at least two courts of justice. One is overseen by the temporal powers of the empire and the other by the eternal power, who is God. In the former court of justice, all may stand, although, in reality only some will; and the worst that can happen there to any accused is "the seeming death of the body." In the latter, however, each must stand, and all, whatever their rank, must render their individual apology; and the worst that can happen there is the "real death, which is reserved for those condemned to the fires of eternity."[83] Erroneous charges against Christianity the Apologists therefore did seek to resist, a task born not only of a desire to defend themselves and their beliefs, but also of their belief that God's will is that all may be saved. So, for them, as they sought to mount their defense against the charge that Christianity was new, and so not true, the apologetic truly was also evangelical.

82. *To Diognetus*, 10.

83. *To Diognetus*, 10. For similar thinking, but in this case in reference to a venerable bishop, see *The Martyrdom of Polycarp*, 11.2, where, on being threatened by the proconsul in Antioch with being burned to death, Polycarp also contrasts "the fire which burns for an hour and, after a little while, is quenched" with "the fire of the judgement to come and . . . the everlasting punishment reserved for the ungodly."

QUESTIONS FOR REFLECTION
AND DISCUSSION

1. In what sense, if any, is Christianity new?

2. In what sense and to what effect may Christians of the twenty-first century maintain with Justin and Theophilos that Moses is *our* prophet, the prophets of the Hebrew Scriptures are *our* teachers, the Hebrew Scriptures are *our* Scriptures, and the people of Israel are *our* ancestors?

3. Is "being passive" and "receptive" a person's proper characteristic, especially when seeking to discern God's self-revelation?

4

ATHEISTS? GUILTY
AS CHARGED

"THAT BEHIND EVERYTHING THAT is made there is a maker" was a commonplace, widely accepted in the second century. In daily life people recognized that behind, for example, a sculpture there was a sculptor and that behind something that moved there was someone, or something, that moved it. In religious life people worked with the same commonplace. Christians, for example, owned the account of the apostle Paul who, speaking in front of the Areopagus, in words that echoed a Stoic formulation, reminded the Athenian crowd assembled before him that in God "we live and move and have our being."[1] In debate with those of other religious persuasions, the Apologists, arguing that the statues of the imperial cults were merely "the work of human hands,"[2] implicitly used the same commonplace. The statues of the imperial cults, they asserted, were not

1. Acts 17:28.
2. Psalm 115:4.

those in whom followers of cults lived and moved and had their being. Rather, these statues were but artefacts of human craftsmen, people who, in turn, were artefacts of the one and only God. Insofar as anything or anyone existed, properly speaking, each lived and moved and had their being only in and through the one Creator of all. In philosophical circles, meanwhile, a more sophisticated form of the same commonplace is to be found. For Greeks assumed that the whole system of numbers originated from the number 1. In their thinking, therefore, there was no "zero." So, philosophers like the Pythagoreans, although not they alone, supposed that the universe's rational order found its source in the rational Monad, a supposition that then prompted others to assume that the artificer, the creative being behind the cosmos, had the characteristics of the Monad. This being, they then concluded, was other than the made world, even as, for example, a painter was other than a painting; and further, they assumed that this being was simple, in marked contrast with the world, which was composed of many, dissoluble parts.

Given such, the common assumption was that behind the world there were gods, "causes" behind that which was "caused," each generally understood as different forms, or manifestations, of one god. So, for example, Aristides readily referred to the gods or god "of the four races of this world's people,"[3] and Justin equally wrote of the religions of the Jews, of the Greeks, and of the Christians. A corollary of such was that the belief that there was no god or gods was then not at all common. Just as in arithmetic there was no "zero," so in theology there was not an absence of a god.

Therefore, when charged with being atheists, the task with which the Apologists saw themselves faced was not that of proving to their accusers that they did believe in a

3. Aristides, *Apology*, 2.

god. Rather, it was that of pointing out both that (i) they in fact were "true theists," those who believed in the only true God, the One who made and moved all, and that (ii) they were "atheists" only in the sense that they denied each and every "false god."

Further, in explaining why they denied the many so-called gods, and affirmed but one God, the Maker and Mover of all things, they saw themselves as not only putting forward an honest and reasonable defense in the face of ignorant and misguided accusations, but also as allowing themselves to be instruments whereby those then erroneously worshipping that which had been made—the statues of the imperial cults and the gods of the Greek poets and dramatists—might mend their ways and turn to the one and only Maker of all that had been made.

ATHEISTS WHEN IT CAME TO THE BELIEF THAT WHAT IS MADE IS DIVINE

Aristides is an example of an Apologist who, when wishing to commend the Christians's understanding of God to a Hellenistic audience, whose myths told of a divine pantheon and whose cults were anything but monotheistic, employed the commonplace that behind every artefact there is an artificer. Drawing his audience's attention to the world in which they lived, he pointed to the fact that it moved. From that he suggested that it was moved, and moved by a being other than itself, indeed, by a being greater than itself. For, he argued, "what moves something is more powerful than what is moved."[4] Then, no doubt influenced by a combination of his Jewish inheritance, especially that aspect which held that God was "one, the Creator of all,"[5] by his

4. Aristides, *Apology*, 1.
5. Aristides, *Apology*, 14.

Christian faith, and by Hellenistic thinking that behind a world composed of many parts there lay a simple Monad, Aristides concluded that there was one God who was "without parts,"[6] the Creator and Mover of the moved and ordered creation of "the heavens and the earth and the sea."[7] So, from a moved, divisible world of many parts Aristides inferred that there was a God, one God and not several, not part of the world, but its Maker and Mover.

Theophilos argued somewhat similarly when he reflected that if a person rightly regarded the cosmos's order and beauty, that person would perceive that "the universe's pilot is God."[8] Indeed, Theophilos was ready to assert that such a person properly should discern the One who "ruled" the world.[9] The verb *kyrieuein*, "to rule," probably here suggested to those versed in both the Greek version of the Hebrew Scriptures, the Septuagint, and the New Testament documents the *Kyrios*, the "Lord" God; and to those acquainted with imperial and cultic titles the same verb may have brought to mind One who challenged the rule of both emperors and the gods to whom a temple had been dedicated.

Tatian's take on this matter was different but consistent. Using, to all intents and purposes as a parable Odysseus's reflection to his rank and file that, since "we cannot all be kings here; and mob rule is a bad thing, . . . let there therefore be one commander only, one king,"[10] Tatian argued that there must be but "a single ruler of the universe."[11] For, behind the ordered multiplicity of the

6. Aristides, *Apology*, 1.

7. Aristides, *Apology*, 1.

8. Theophilos, *To Autolycus*, 1.5.

9. Theophilos, *To Autolycus*, 2.10.

10. Homer, *Iliad* 2.203–5.

11. Tatian, *Address*, 29.2.

universe, Tatian held, there must be one who ordered and, when necessary, will restore order. Noteworthy, moreover, especially in the light of what being accused of atheism then meant, is Tatian's conclusion that there must be *one* ruler, as opposed to *many* rulers, of the universe, and *not* that there must be one ruler, as opposed to *no* ruler. For Tatian, as for those many others influenced by the assumption that the whole system of numbers originated from the number 1, theologically there was no "zero." Theologically "no ruler" was an impossibility. There *had* to be a ruler, and *only one* ruler. Only the individual who very foolishly wholly misread the made and moved world could and would say in his heart, there is no god.[12]

Given then that what was created was not divine, the Apologists were adamant in maintaining that human beings—emperors and Hadrian's deified favorite, Antinous, included—were not divine, and so were not to be worshipped.[13] Nor were prayers to be offered *to* them.

Prayer *for* emperors was, however, a different matter, as was the honoring of emperors as human beings appointed by God to carry out God's will for the empire. So, Theophilos, for example, echoing the apostle Paul's thinking, wrote that emperors were people who had been appointed by God to maintain right, to counter all that hindered the general peace and prosperity of the empire, and to judge everyone justly, each and all of these imperial responsibilities to be carried out in accordance with God's will as revealed especially in the Law and Prophets of the Hebrew Scriptures.[14] These self-same emperors, who had been appointed to so a great task, were, yet, as Theophilos

12. See Psalm 14:1; 53:1.

13. See Justin, *Apology*, 1.29; Theophilos, *To Autolycus*, 3.8; Athenagoras, *Plea*, 30.2

14. Theophilos, *To Autolycus*, 1.11. See also Romans 13:1–3.

further stated, fallible human beings. While therefore they rightly deserved the people's prayers and obedience as and when they legislated in accordance with God's will, they were not to be surprised, if and when they legislated not in accordance with God's will, to be faced with a judicious resistance. Such resistance was born of a faithfulness on the part of Christians to God, a faithfulness intended, among other things, to prompt the emperors and their ministers to mend their ways and again to legislate as God willed.

Similarly, the Apologists insisted that the sun, the moon, and the stars, which long had been believed by adherents to the empire's cosmic religions to rule the affairs of earth, were made and so not divine;[15] and, in insisting so, they dismissed the practicing of astrology and, indirectly, invited people to step back from being ruled by celestial bodies and step forward to acknowledging the care extended to them by the very One who made those self-same lights of heaven.

It was, however, in and through their non-participation in the various cultic practices of the empire that Christians found themselves especially faced with the possibility of being accused of being atheists. Not surprisingly therefore the Apologists particularly turned their attention to the matter of religious statues and the sacrifices associated with them. Their arguments, at times, were *ad hominem*. Statues, they urged, had been made, sometimes of the meanest matter, only then, sometimes, to be remade into yet something else—a bronze vessel might be melted down, made into a statue to be worshipped, only then to be melted down again, to be remade yet again, perhaps this time into another kitchen item.[16] This was hardly a dignified origin

15. See Theophilos, *To Autolycus*, 2.35.

16. See, for example, *To Diognetus*, 2 and also Justin, *Apology*, 1.9, where it is remarked that "out of vessels of dishonour . . . [people]

or destiny for something to be worshipped. When still a statue, they often were offered blood and steaming fats, despite the fact that the stench of such offerings was unbearable to most reasonable persons. Indeed, it was suggested, had such fats been offered to a human being, they would have been received not as a mark of honor but as an insult. Some statues, the Apologists continued, were treated with care while others were not. Earthenware or stone statues were left unattended, by both day and night, while statues made of silver and gold, as though unable to protect themselves, were guarded by day and locked away by night. All the statues, and not just some, the Apologists then further observed, rotted and wasted away. Such arguments may present themselves as *ad hominem*. Yet, undergirding these arguments were more serious theological themes. That which was melted down and refashioned was *changeable and inconstant*, in contrast with the One who is unchangeable and ever constant. To the statues blood and fat were offered, whereas to God bloodless sacrifices of thankful praise, common prayer, the Eucharist, and a righteous life properly were to be given,[17] even though these, while delighted in, yet were *not necessary*. For, unlike anything made, God is not dependent upon anything or anyone. Nothing is necessary for the Creator of all. Perhaps, most important is the argument that the statues eventually rotted and wasted away. Their *finitude* was therein exposed, as was their being the very antithesis of the truly infinite, imperishable God. Moreover, in their being unable to preserve themselves, their *inability to preserve and safeguard their worshippers* was also made manifest. Given such, there is, the Apologists seemly suggested, a pointlessness in

---

make what they call a god."

17. See Justin, *Apology*, 1.10; Justin, *Dialogue with Trypho*, 117; 118.2; Justin, *Apology* 1.65–66.

agreeing to demands that all people should offer sacrifices to the statues of the imperial cults. Such sacrifices were supposedly to secure, in public life, the *pax Romana* (peace of Rome), through a winning the *pax deorum* (peace of the gods), and, at a home's *lararium* (the domestic shrine where the *paterfamilias* led his family and its servants in offering sacrifices to their household guardian deities), a family's safety and prosperity. There is also implied in such sacrifices a disregard for, even a dishonoring of, the One God whom the Christians faithfully worship, the one and only source of peace and safety.

For all the above *ad hominem* arguments, with their possible theological implications, the main argument that the Apologists advanced against the worship of the statues of the imperial cult was that which depended on such psalms as Psalm 135. The statues, the Apologists observed, had mouths, but could not speak; they had eyes, but, unlike the all-seeing God, they could not see.[18] In short, they were lifeless, made by a person who, in turn, was lifeless but for the fact that he or she had been given life by God, the Maker of all people. Statues were, therefore, the *most derivative,* of all that was made the *least worthy* to be honored.

Apologists like Theophilos took this argument further. For he not only drew on the conclusions born of noting that the statues, though having mouths and eyes, were dumb and blind, but also, attending to a following verse from Psalm 135, namely that "they that make [*sc.* statues] are like them | and so are all they that put their trust in them,"[19] suggested that the makers and worshippers of the statues of the imperial cults had also become like the statues that they worshipped. The makers and worshippers of

18. See, for example, Aristides, *Apology*, 13 and *To Diognetus*, 2.4–5.

19. Psalm 135:18.

the statues had mouths. Yet they had become dumb when it came to praising the Maker of all. They had eyes. Yet they saw neither the error of their ways nor the one, true God.[20] This latter point is all the more poignant when it is remembered that the Apologists, bar none, held that the visible and the invisible were intertwined. For they believed that it belonged to everyone to look upon the made, visible world, to search for meaning—not to create meaning, as the makers of statues did in making gods in their own image—and to discern in and through the visible world the invisible Maker of all.

The links between that which was made and the Maker, the Apologists believed, were there. They but needed to be discerned, a discerning that was open to all as this discernment was dependent on, not intellectual ability, but the eyes of the purified soul. Indeed, Justin stressed that point in his assertion that God's Word, the Logos *spermatikos*, had sown in everyone the "seed of divine knowledge."[21] So everyone had been granted the possibility of discerning the true God, enabled "to speak well [of the Truth] in proportion to the share each had of the Logos *spermatikos*,"[22] and called to live "reasonably"—"reasonably" meaning "in accordance with the Logos, God's Reason." This point Theophilos and Athenagoras further underscored when

20. See Theophilos, *To Autolycus*, 1.10.

21. Justin, *Apology*, 2.8.1–3; 2.13.3–5. Justin had adapted Stoic thinking that the *logos spermatikos*, the generative reason or power, was that by which all was produced from primary fire as from seed. It was the creative force in nature, forming the universe in general and individual things in particular. He had also reworked the Stoic understanding that the *logoi spermatikoi* were the generative powers of the soul. See also Justin, *Dialogue with Trypho*, 3.7, where Justin echoes Plato's affirmation in *Timaeus* 52A that the deity is discernible to the human mind.

22. Justin, *Apology*, 2.13.

they wrote, respectively, that the eyes of the purified soul could see God[23] and that by thought and mind the transcendent God could be contemplated.[24]

In summary, the Apologists argued that people should worship the Maker of all and not anything that the Maker had made. The thinking here clearly is that one ought not to dishonor God, a point explicitly made when Aristides wrote that things made have been made "for the honor of God almighty."[25] Maybe, however, there is here, alongside this sense of the impropriety of dishonoring *God* in and though honoring the made instead of the Maker, a further sense of the wretchedness of dishonoring *that which has been made*, where "that which has been made" includes not only matter as made into statues but also matter understood as *those who make and worship statues*. For, implicit in the writings of the various Apologists, there is the thinking that matter is dishonored when, in contravention to its being allowed naturally to point to its Maker, it is forcibly fashioned into a statue which only diverts its worshipper from true to false worship. And there is further the thought that the maker of the statue and its worshipper are dishonored, or rather, bring dishonor on themselves, in the very acts of the making and then worshipping the manufactured statues. Put differently, in making idols and in becoming an idolater, people dishonor not only God but also *creation*, both in the form of matter as and when made into statues to be worshipped, and of human beings themselves.

What certainly lie behind the injunction not to exchange the worship of the Maker for that which has been made are the thoughts both that Christians rightly should desist from any acts that dishonor the Maker of all things

23. Theophilos, *To Autolycus*, 1.2.

24. Athenagoras, *Plea*, 4.1; 10.1.

25. Aristides, *Apology*, 13.

and that those of other cults should desist from demanding that anyone, Christians included, should offer sacrifices, libations, and the like to the gods of the imperial cult. For, it was held, such rituals and rites did not placate the gods and so did not usher in the *pax deorum* with its hoped-for *pax Romana*. Rather, these Greco-Roman cultic practices dishonored, as people like Aristides maintained, the one and only God, and led to "wars and famines and deprivations of all things,"[26] hallmarks of divine judgement and the very opposite of the longed-for peace.

So, the Apologists advocated, everyone should join with Christians in honoring the one God who both had made all for humanity's sake and ever willed to bless all that God had made. It was for these several reasons that Christians did not believe in the "gods" of the empire and abstained from the cults associated with them. In that sense Christians were indeed "atheists," guilty as charged.

ATHEISTS ALSO WHEN IT CAME TO THE BELIEF THAT THE GODS OF THE POETS AND DRAMATISTS WERE DIVINE

The Apologists generally were aware of the thinking of the pagan philosopher Euhemerus [d.250 BC], who maintained that the lives and actions of the gods of the Hellenistic myths were to be explained by reference to mere mortals and long past historical events. Tatian quoted Metrodorus of Lampsacus, who, using allegory as a hermeneutical tool, understood Homeric deities such as Hera, Athena, and Zeus as but "natural substances and arrangements of elements."[27] Meanwhile, Justin, Tatian, and Athenagoras were aware of the reasoning of Socrates and Plato, the former of whom

26. Aristides, *Apology*, 8.
27. Tatian, *Address*, 21.3.

Justin judged to be a "Christian before Christ,"[28] one of those philosophers who held that the gods of the Homeric epics were but figments of the imagination,[29] whose fictitious lives were anything but worthy of the title "divine."[30]

The general conclusions that the gods of the poets and dramatists were not divine the Apologists shared, although primarily for two other main reasons. Firstly, deeming that it was improper to worship that which was made rather than the Maker, they also deemed it improper to worship "gods" fashioned by poets and dramatists, who themselves had been fashioned by the Creator of all. The "gods" of the poets and dramatists, they held, were but *creations of creatures of the Creator*, literary compositions of humans created by the one, divine Maker of all.

Secondly, the Apologists argued that the lives of the gods of the Greek poems and plays often were marked by adultery and strife, thief and parricide, behavior so ungodlike that it contradicted any claim to godliness and so wicked that, had such been that practiced by humans, it rightly would have resulted in, not approbation, but prosecution—an argument not so dissimilar from that advanced by philosophy. Socrates, as Justin approvingly maintained, had sought to "cast out from the state both Homer and the rest of the poets and had taught people to reject . . . those who did the things which the poets related."[31] In theological terms, the Apologists therefore asserted, the divinity of such "gods" could not reasonably be sustained and, for both theological and moral reasons, their behavior should not be imitated. For imitating such behavior both did injustice

28. Justin, *Apology*, 1.46. See also. Justin, *Apology*, 2.13.

29. Justin, *Apology*, 1.23.

30. See Justin, *Apology*, 2.5.4–6; Tatian, *Address*, 10.2–3; Athenagoras, *Plea*, 17.2; 19.1; 21.1.

31. Justin, *Apology*, 2.10.

to the Holy One and caused moral damage to not only the devotees of these "gods" but also to any uncritical observers of such devotions. As Aristides, having listed the moral failings of the gods of the Greeks, reflected, "all people have taken occasion to do all wicked and impure things, and so the whole world has been corrupted."[32]

Not all the Apologists employed the philosophical argument that behind the many there is the One, that in a dissonant world there is One who is the ultimate touchstone by which the harmonious and the disharmonious are distinguished, and that behind all behavior there is One who is very good, who is the judge between the good and the shameful. Tatian did, however, employ such an argument. He drew the attention of his readers to the Greek philosophical schools, with both their various, contradictory teachings and their distinct followers who quarreled one with another.[33] He reminded his readers that in Greek society "there are as many codes of laws as there are types of cities, so that things which amongst some are deemed shameful are thought to be good amongst others."[34] Tatian's argument here, however, was not that Christianity therefore ought to have been tolerated as yet one more "school" among the many other differing and often contradictory schools of philosophy. His argument was rather that the agreement between Christians demonstrated Christianity's truth whilst the disagreement between the various philosophical schools and the cities advocating different moral practices evidenced Greek society's errors. How unreasonable then, Tatian asserted, was the society that, though continually damaged by its tolerated divisions, yet sought to "oppose [sc. Christians] who [sc.

32. Aristides, *Apology*, 11.

33. Tatian, *Address*, 25.2.

34. Tatian, *Address*, 28.1.

agreed] amongst themselves"[35] and had "one common way of life."[36] Of equal importance with Tatian's seeking here to "convert" his readers from harassing Christians was his desire to persuade his audience to worship the God of the Christians. For his argument here also sought to draw the attention of his readers not to a Christian version of the Greek idea of *Themis*—that powerful principle of right that lay beyond and behind the pantheon of the empire's cults and theaters and against which the behavior of their followers was to be judged—nor to a Holy One amongst other Holy Ones, but to *the* Holy One, the *one and only* God revealed to all and worshipped by Christians, the sole Judge of all that is discordant and immoral and the one and only Source of all harmony and holiness. In short, Tatian's goal seems to have been not primarily to persuade people not to attack Christians, nor to adopt the Christian religion, but to worship the one God of the Christians. The former two would, it would seem that Tatian thought, follow if and when the third was realized.

Some thirty years earlier Aristides introduced a very different argument against worshipping the various gods of the Greek poems and dramas. He invited his readers to note that the gods of the poets and dramatists could not preserve themselves. Then, having given people time to reflect upon that observation, he enquired, "How then can [*sc.* these gods] protect and save their worshippers?"[37] In short, he was asking his readers to note a serious soteriological corollary of the frailty of these gods. Aristides cited many examples of the frailty of these gods, but he nearly always concluded his citations with a refrain along the lines of, if the god is not able to help itself, how can it help others? One example will

35. Tatian, *Address*, 25.2.

36. Tatian, *Address*, 28.1.

37. Aristides, *Apology*, 13.

suffice here. Adonis, Aristides noted, gored by a wild boar, was unable to help himself and so died. "If Adonis was unable to help himself, how," Aristides asked, "is he able to care for humanity?"[38] Aristides's question was no idle question for mid-second-century people, who thought that demons and devils were everywhere, seeking people's harm, and that death, like the sword of Damocles, hung uncertainly over every head, ready to fall at any moment. In the midst of such everyday uncertainty, people's believing that a god, strong to save, was with and for them was unsurprisingly of paramount importance and of great comfort. It was the source of hopeful confidence.

Certainly it must be acknowledged that Aristides's sense of a constantly almighty God and of the weakness of matter are not early examples of the arguments that creatures cannot save fellow creatures and that only very God can save securely. It must, however, also be acknowledged that Aristides's thinking here is not inconsistent with such arguments marshalled in, for example, the fourth-century anti-Arian debates. Yet, whatever the connection, if any, between the mid-to-late second-century and early fourth-century soteriological arguments, the fragility of the gods of Hellenistic culture and their inability to endure was, for Aristides, a strong argument against these gods being trustworthy and true.

QUESTIONS FOR REFLECTION AND DISCUSSION

1. To acknowledge that all people are creatures is a great leveler. If embraced, are there then ways in which society, from the greatest of its members to the very least, should now remodel itself?

38. Aristides, *Apology*, 11.

2. The Apologists often prioritized a creature-centered over an anthropocentric understanding of humanity. When people are viewed firstly, but not exclusively, as creatures, do environmental issues take on a sharper perspective? And does care for the environment cease to be optional?

3. If God alone can save and even the most laudable human thought and action cannot, what is to be made of the suggestion that people are to "work out [their] own salvation, with fear and trembling"?[39]

4. The Apologists argued strongly against the worship of matter. When nowadays people, for example, "read their stars," are they acting improperly in worshipping matter, or simply engaging in "innocent fun," against which it is not worth arguing?

---

39. See Philippians 2:12.

5

ATHEISTS?—NOT GUILTY AS CHARGED

The mid-to-late second-century Apologists openly admitted that they did not and would not sacrifice to either cultic statues or emperors. Given that, they were very ready to plead guilty to the accusation of being "atheists." At the same time, however, they were adamant that they would not forsake their allegiance to the One whom they believed to be the only true God, whose very monotheistic existence prompted their "atheism" when it came to deities of the Greco-Roman cults and cultures. Given that, they also were therefore anything but ready to plead guilty to a charge of being "atheists." Depending on the context, the Apologists either were "atheists" or were anything but "atheists"; or, put differently, they were theists, but only when the god in question was the God of Christianity.

THEISTS CERTAINLY

Aristides, the earliest of these Apologists, was influenced by his Jewish inheritance, especially that aspect which held that God was "one, the Creator of all,"[1] by his Christian faith and by the Hellenistic thought that behind a world composed of many parts there lay a simple Monad. Not surprisingly then, having reflected upon a moved, divisible, multi-part world, composed of "the heavens and the earth and the sea,"[2] he concluded that God was "not begotten, not made; of a constant nature, without beginning and without end; immortal, complete and incomprehensible."[3] An initial impression from the use by Aristides of such epithets, which state what God is *not*, may be that he thought of God as distant and other. Such an impression could find some confirmation in the negative terminology of the contemporary Middle Platonism, the Stoicized form that Platonism had assumed from the beginning of the first century BC, which worked with a clearer sense of a transcendent god than Plato had and which was increasingly to become a significant intellectual background to the thinking of both Hellenistic Jews such as Philo and many early church thinkers. Indeed, such an impression could appear to find further confirmation in that Aristides did not refer to God as "Father," not even in the sense of the "Father of all," whether of people or of things. Not to use the title "Father" as applied to the Trinity might be expected at that time; but not to use the title "Father of all" as applied even to God's people, especially when it had been used by both Jesus and the disciples whom the same Jesus had taught to pray, may be surprising. That said, that initial impression may be wrong. For

1. Aristides, *Apology*, 14.
2. Aristides, *Apology*, 1.
3. Aristides, *Apology*, 1.

in using these negative (apophatic) epithets, Aristides may not have been aiming to suggest that God was distant and other, but rather that God was essentially distinct from the world of matter. By his using seemingly deliberately chosen contrasting epithets of matter and of God—the world had been made, was divisible and the like, while God was *not* made, was *in*divisible, and the like—Aristides, rather than meaning to suggest that God was "distant" from the world of matter, may have been seeking to *distinguish* matter from God, that which should not be worshipped from that which alone should be worshipped. This was a not inappropriate agenda when a central issue at stake was whether or not the statues of the various Hellenistic cults should be worshipped. Indeed, that Aristides's employing these negative epithets of God ought not to be read as suggesting that he intended God to be understood as a distant God finds support in his further titling God as the Mover and Maker of all. When the apophatic epithets, so interpreted to describe God, are juxtaposed with Aristides's repeated calling God the "Mover" and "Maker" of all, his announcing that God made all "for the sake of humanity,"[4] and his complimenting the Jews for rightly serving the "one God, the Creator of all, the Almighty,"[5] Aristides's belief that God was not solitary and unrelated to the world of matter becomes evident. Aristides's God certainly is distinct from but is *not alien to* the made, mutable, and mortal world, even as that world is distinct from but should not be alien to its Creator.

The anonymous writer of the *Letter to Diognetus* argued to much the same end as Aristides, but in a somewhat less obviously philosophical style. He too described God in contradistinction with the made, visible world. For, for apologetic reasons, he too was seeking to distinguish the

4. Aristides, *Apology*, 1.
5. Aristides, *Apology*, 14.

Maker, who alone is to be worshipped, from that made, and which, being made, is not to be worshipped. So the letter writer described God as the invisible Maker of all, a making effected in and through the Demiurge, or "Craftsman," a title once used by Plato to describe the creator of the immortal soul and which recalls the "master workman" of the Book of the Proverbs.[6] By mentioning this Craftsman, who was at one and the same time both *distinct from* and yet *connected with* the Maker of all that God had made, the letter writer sought to distinguish but not to divide the invisible Maker from all that had been made.

Indeed, lest his reader might be tempted to understand the letter writer's God as solitary, the letter writer called upon his readers to reflect upon God's involvement in that made. For, in stating that God was the Maker of all, the letter writer wished his reader to note more than a general statement about who the Creator was. So, he wrote that "the Lord and Maker of the world . . . made all things and determined the proper place of each,"[7] therein pointing beyond God's making of all to God's concern for all particular things, even each's "proper place."

The same sense of divine attention to the particular and contingent is evidenced elsewhere. Alluding to the creation and redemption narratives, the letter writer referred to God the "Father,"[8] "Father" in the sense of "Father of all," one who so loved humanity that God made the world for humanity's sake, formed people in God's own image, and placed everything in their care. The same letter writer

6. See, for example, Plato, *Timaeus* 41C. See also Plato, *Timaeus* 90A and Proverbs 8:22, 30 where the Lord is described as having created wisdom "at the beginning of his works," who then was "beside [the Lord], like a master workman."

7. *To Diognetus*, 8.7.

8. *To Diognetus*, 10.1.

described God as having sent to humanity his only-begotten Son and as having promised people the kingdom of heaven.[9] In his treatment of both the timing and the manner of the incarnation the letter writer yet further emphasized God's relationship with the particular world that he had made. To God's mercy and goodness, exhibited in the incarnation, we shall return. Suffice it for the moment to note how the powerless, saved by the Savior's power, are to look upon God "as Nurse, Father, Teacher, Counsellor, Healer, Mind, Light, Honor, Glory, Might and Life."[10] These titles certainly are rich in their describing God's concurrent sovereign and yet intimate relationship of concern with the people of all sorts and conditions of the world.

Theophilos, while writing some twenty to twenty-five years after Aristides, was mindful, as Aristides had been, that God in his radical transcendence was essentially unknowable and inexpressible. So Theophilos also resorted, at times, to a negative, or apophatic, way of speaking of God, describing God not in terms of who God *is* but of who God is *not*. "In glory," Theophilos wrote, in words that echoed the language of worship as much as that of apophaticism, God "is uncontainable, in greatness incomprehensible, in loftiness inconceivable, in strength beyond understanding, in wisdom unteachable, in goodness inimitable and in beneficence inexpressible."[11] Theophilos's aim seems to be not to describe God as solitary but as *unique*.

Yet Theophilos's God is not unique in the sense of being one of a class of gods, albeit the Highest God. Nor is his God unique in the sense of being the most glorious, or greatest, or wisest, as judged in comparison with other gods and as measured against such a principle as that of

9. *To Diognetus*, 10.2.

10. *To Diognetus*, 9.6.

11. Theophilos, *To Autolycus*, 1.3.

Themis, the ancient Greek principle that, it was believed, lay beyond and behind everything, and against which all were judged to be, for example, "glorious" or "great" or "wise." If anything, Theophilos's God *is* that "*Themis*," the one against whom a person is judged to be "glorious" or "great" or "wise," against whom individual behavior is judged to be "meet and right." Further, Theophilos's God is "inimitable in goodness" and so unlike the Zeus of the Greek myths. For, as Theophilos argued, if Zeus is here, he is not there; and as he is therefore not everywhere, he is not able to help and care for all at all times and in every place.[12] God, as understood by Theophilos, is, however, everywhere, ever present, constantly bestowing his goodness and providential care on each and all; or, as Theophilos said, God is "inimitable in goodness," where "goodness" is viewed in terms not only of quality but also extent of application.

In summary, it is not that Theophilos wanted to stress the "otherness" of God at the expense of the "immediacy" of God. It is rather that, in keeping with his belief that "God is not contained, but is himself the *locus* of the universe"—for otherwise "the place containing [God] would be greater than [God], since what contains is greater than what is contained"[13]—Theophilos used such apophatic titles as "uncontainable," "infinite," and the like to stress a God who is illimitable, neither open to being comprehended or possessed by the human mind, nor "hedged in" by a finite world, as though he was "contained" by time and space. This God, by very definition, is the God *of all*, and *for all*.

Maybe, however, it is Justin, who, of all the mid-to-late second-century Apologists, gives us the fullest theological picture of both the oneness of God, in contradistinction with

12. Theophilos, *To Autolycus*, 2.3.

13. Theophilos, *To Autolycus*, 2.3. See also Theophilos, *To Autolycus*, 2.22; Athenagoras, *Plea*, 8.4.

the pluralistic theologies of the Hellenistic cults, and of the world's standing in the face of that one and only God.

Against a background, common to all the Apologists, of cults that worshipped statues ("that which has been made," by any other name) and of the various Hellenistic poems and dramas, which had domesticated the Greek world's pantheon, Justin aimed to lift the eyes of his readers to a theology in which there was only one God, the Highest, who alone properly deserved to be worshipped. As a corollary, he further urged that this one God was "the Maker of all," an "all" of which not even a single part could be worshipped without a slipping into idolatry. In practical terms, this meant that, amongst other items made, the statues and images of the imperial cult should not be worshipped, not even *in extremis*. Nor needed they to be, not even when external powers threatened the empire's internal security and prosperity. For *God*—being one God, the Maker of all—was the source of all, peace and goodness included. The empire was therefore horribly mistaken in thinking that the peace of the empire emanated from the *pax deorum*, won by all people's observant participation in the sacrificial rites of the imperial cults. Rather, the empire's peace lay in the *pax Dei*, unearned and given freely by the one God, in whom alone lay all people's security.

So, in terms reminiscent of the rather distinct, negative vocabulary of Middle Platonism, with its emerging conception of the transcendence of God, Justin described God as one, without beginning, unmoved, incomprehensible, illimited and illimitable. This same God, he also described, but this time in terms reminiscent of the language of the Scriptures, as God, the Maker and Father of all. In language drawn from *both* a negative theology *and* a theology replete with positive affirmations, language *both* apophatic *and* kataphatic, Justin sought to remind his audience in Rome that God was the only God, that "above [God] there is no other god,"[14] and that all else that exists exists in and through the one God.

In language accommodated to a more Hellenistic audience and to one raised in the synagogue Justin therefore sought to press home the point that Christians were *not atheists*. They trusted in one God, who, being not a solitary God, nor one unconcerned with, nor alien to the world of matter, could not be disregarded even when the empire, *in extremis*, called upon all to participate in universal sacrifice that the anger of the imperial gods might be placated. The better choice, or, more accurately, the *only* choice rightly to be made, Justin concluded, was then to be true to the one God and face the possibility of being martyred by a threatened empire. For the alternative, namely that of offering sacrifices to non-existent gods, in the vain hope of winning a *pax deorum* and so earning the *pax Romana*, was both ineffective and a betrayal of the sole source of peace and concord, God the Creator and Sustainer of all.

Justin's beliefs that God was one and that through God's Logos all was made raised questions that Justin neither could nor did seek to avoid. These questions included, if God made all through his Logos, and neither God nor the Logos were created, were both divine? and, if they were both divine, did that amount to a compromising, if not a denying monotheism? Had Trypho, Justin's Jewish interlocutor, been someone who did not hold the Hebrew Scriptures in high regard, there would have been no point in Justin beginning his answers to such questions in the Scriptures; but Trypho was a Jew, for whom the Scriptures, when rightly interpreted, were "authoritative." So, Justin began forming his answers to the above questions by referring Trypho to the creation narrative in the book of

14. Justin, *Dialogue with Trypho*, 56.

Genesis, and, in particular, to the text, "let us make humanity . . . ."[15] Justin was not prepared to allegorize the text. He
knew that Trypho, by religion a Jew and by set of mind
a Hellenist, would admit that a "maker" was superior to
"that made." So Justin highlighted two words from the text,
"us" and "make," and argued that the word "us" suggested
a plurality of makers, and that these "makers," not having
been "made," must be "divine." The Hebrew Scriptures, Justin urged Trypho, when rightly interpreted, authoritatively
pointed to a plurality within the one Godhead.

Justin's conclusion led, however, to a further question: if the Logos was not made and was therefore divine,
and if—as suggested by Genesis's "let us make humanity
. . ."—there was indeed a plurality in the godhead, how was
the "us" to be understood? How was the relationship of the
Logos with God to be explained in such a way as would
be deemed consistent with believing that God was one? In
reply, Justin referred Trypho to two particular understandings of the Logos. The first understanding again drew upon
the Hebrew Scriptures and the second upon Stoic thinking, Greek philosophy certainly, yet philosophy not entirely
antithetical to a Trypho's mind. The first, Justin held, maintained that the Logos was the "Son" of God and the second,
that he was the "Mind" or "Thought" of God.

Having discussed the Genesis text, "let us make humanity . . . ," Justin pointed Trypho to another Hebrew text,
namely Proverbs 8:22, "the Lord created me [sc. the Logos]
the beginning of his ways for his works." Immediately, however, Justin replaced the verb "created," firstly, with "established" and then with "begat." Thus: "before he formed the
earth . . . and the depths, before the springs of water came
forth, before the mountains were settled, before all the hills,"

15. Genesis 1:26.

Justin wrote, "he *begat* me."[16] Then, drawing upon this shift in vocabulary, he argued that "this Offspring was begotten by the Father before all created things"[17]—the contrast between the Offspring, the Logos, having been "begotten" and all things having been "created," and their respective essential distinctiveness, now the more marked.

Interestingly, only three chapters earlier, Justin had referred to the Logos as "God, the Son of the only, unbegotten, unutterable God."[18] When that is set alongside Justin's assertion that "the one begotten is numerically distinct from the one who begets,"[19] there would appear to be here a recognition of and an attempt by Justin to persuade Trypho also to recognize—on the grounds of Jewish sacred texts and common sense (for, Justin implied, one begotten cannot be numerically the same of the begetter)—both the *divinity of the Logos* and an acceptable *plurality in the Godhead*, a divine Begetter and a divine Begotten, both the makers of all things.

Clearly Justin did not, as later church fathers did, attend to the theological subtleties possible in regard to essential commonality and essential distinction when parties are related, the one to the other, on the one hand, as "begetter" and "begotten" and, on the other, as "Maker" and "that made." That said, there is, in Justin's attending to the filial

16. Justin, *Dialogue with Trypho*, 129. See also Justin, *Dialogue with Trypho*, 61–62. The italics are mine.

17. Justin, *Dialogue with Trypho*, 129.

18. Justin, *Dialogue with Trypho*, 126.

19. Justin, *Dialogue with Trypho*, 129. The composer of the *Letter to Diognetus* does write of the "Father" and "his Child," even his "beloved Child" [*To Diognetus*, 8.9, 11]. The language, however, seems to allude to the gospel narratives concerning Christ as God's obedient "beloved son" of the baptism narratives [see Mark 1:11 and parallels], rather than to the essential relation of the Father and his Logos.

relation of the Logos to God, an attempt to address the matter of plurality within the one deity.

The second significant understanding of the Logos, expressed less in Jewish and more in Hellenistic forms, was that which saw the Logos as God's Mind or Reason. In a brief and far from systematic way, Justin drew upon the Stoics's all important anthropological distinction between the *logos endiathetos*, a person's innate rationality, and the *logos prophorikos*, the self-same person's innate rationality, but now extrapolated, or made known, whether by speech or any other means of self-expression. Adapting this thinking to his own end, Justin posited that the Logos *endiathetos* was God's Reason or Mind, while the Logos *prophorikos* was God's Reason or Mind willingly expressed, most notably in the acts of creation and revelation. Justin posited such, however, without in any way wanting to suggest that in and through such self-expression either God was diminished, the result of the thought's "departure" on being uttered, or the Logos was aggrandized, the Logos in some sense becoming somehow "more" once the Logos had been expressed. In the acts of creation and revelation there was, for Justin, neither division nor multiplication. In being uttered the Logos was not divided from God, so leaving God "Mind-less." Nor did the one God somehow then become two. Even as Logos *prophorikos*, the Logos remained ever God's Mind or Reason, God's Logos *endiathetos*. What plurality-in-unity there was in God "before" God's creating all things and self-revealing, there was "after" such creating and self-revealing.

Interestingly, Theophilos also employed the idea of the Logos being *endiathetos*, and, for the sake of creating and self-revealing, *prophorikos*, of which the image of human "thought" then "expressed" as a human word was analogous. He too was ready to assert that God was not diminished in and through the Logos having been expressed. Yet, whereas Justin drew upon the image of a fire kindled from a fire, the latter in no manner having been diminished in and through its kindling the former, Theophilos employed the example of a word, or thought spoken—the Logos, God's Word or Reason or Thought, once "expressed," did not leave God "wordless," or "without Reason."[20] As in Justin's case, so in Theophilos's, the primary emphasis was centered around the question of whether or not God was diminished by God's Logos having been expressed. Yet, in the assertion that the Logos, once expressed, did not leave God "wordless," without a Logos, there may also be an anticipation of the later belief that God's begetting the Son is an *eternal begetting*, a belief integral to that of the eternal relationship of God and the Logos, the Son.

Indeed, an incipient form of that belief may perhaps be found in Book 2.10 of Theophilos's *Letter to Autolycus*, where Theophilos touched upon the contrast of what is "generated" (*ta gegenēmena*), namely matter, with the One who is "ingenerate" (*agenētos*), namely God, who "begat" (*egennēsen*) his own Logos, for the purpose of creating all things. There is there a contrast, which was developed and made more explicit in time,[21] between, on the one hand, what, is "generated," "what came into being," namely creation, and, on the other hand, the One who is "ingenerate," God, with whom the Logos is most intimately associated, "being innate [*endiathetos*] in God's own deepest,

---

20. Theophilos, *To Autolycus*, 2,10; 2.22. See also Justin, *Dialogue with Trypho*, 61 and Justin, *Dialogue with Trypho*, 128.

21. See, for example, Athanasius, *A Defence of the Nicene Definition*, 10 and *Against the Arians*, 3.61 and 1.58. This later development refers, however, primarily to the relation of the Father and Son, rather than, as here, to that of the Son and all created things.

innermost being."[22] Moreover, there is there also the distinguishing between the Logos whom God "begat" and matter which God "generated"—the verb, "to beget," used of the Logos but not of matter, and the verb, "to be generated," used of matter but not here of the Logos, possibly suggesting some sense of a filial relationship between God and the Logos whom God "begat" in order that the world might be "generated" or "made."

That said, if there is here a hint of the filial relationship of God and the Logos, it is only a *possible hint*. For the references to the ingenerate God and the begotten Logos probable are more generally to be viewed within the wider context of God the Creator and all that God has made. For, for apologetic reasons, Theophilos overwhelmingly wrote against the worshipping of matter in any shape or form. So, for example, Theophilos was very ready to write of creation, that which is generated, as being not "co-eternal with God," and so not to be worshipped, in contrast with the Logos who, it may be inferred, is *co-eternal* and so *rightly to be worshipped*. Equally, Theophilos was also ready to assert that what is "generated" is needy, whilst what is "ingenerate" lacks nothing. Again, although it is only implied, it yet is here implied that God, the ingenerate One, therefore never lacked anything, not even the Logos. It is another way of Theophilos's implying that the Logos is co-eternal with God, and so to be worshipped. Theophilos may have hinted at the filial relation of God and the Logos. He more than hinted, however, at the co-eternity of the Logos with God, a co-eternity wanting to all that had been brought into being and that therefore could be worshipped only improperly.

22. Theophilos, *To Autolycus*, 2.10. The noun here translated as "deepest, innermost being," when used of a human family, bears the sense of "one's own flesh and blood."

Athenagoras employed a variant upon Theophilos's distinction of "ingenerate" and "generated." Arguing that the gods of the Homeric myths were not gods, he engaged with the practice of philosophers like Plato of contrasting the verb "to be" [*einai*] with the verb "to become," or "to come into being" [*gignesthai*] and their respective cognates. For, for these philosophers, "what *is*" is "what *eternally* is" while "what comes into being" is not "what eternally is." For the latter, that which comes into being, has a beginning. So, Athenagoras concluded, the gods of the Homeric myths, which had come into being, were "what never *is*,[23] . . . [but were] created, having a beginning and an end." By implication, he further concluded, the God of the Christians, the Source of all, "always is and [did] not come into being . . . [and is] uncreated."[24] In short, Athenagoras, at least in this regard, virtually identified the Christian God with the Platonic deity, who simply "is," and so is neither "generated" nor "perishable."[25]

More generally, however, Athenagoras employed language more akin to that of Justin and Theophilos. Hence, he described the Father as the author of all. The Son is God's inseparable, eternal Mind. Yet the Son is also he who issues from God, being the "first begotten," "first begotten" in the sense, not of being the first of all things to come into being, but of having been made "the beginning of God's ways for God's works."[26] The Spirit, Athenagoras mean-

---

23 In line with the philosophical language of Plato, "what never is" here signifies what is *contingent*, in contrast with "what *is*," which identifies what is self-existent, dependent on nothing beyond itself to exist.

24. Athenagoras, *Plea*, 19.2. See also Plato, *Timaeus* 27D.

25. Athenagoras, *Plea*, 19.1.

26. Athenagoras, *Plea*, 10.4, referring to Proverbs 8:22.

while wrote, is an "effluence" from God, which is active in those who spoke prophetically.[27]

Athenagoras was therefore ready to speak of God's *oneness*. So he wrote of "the unity [*henotēs*] of the Son with the Father, . . . the communion [*koinōnia*] of the Father with the Son, . . . of the union [*henōsis*] of the Spirit, the Son and the Father, and of the diversity [*diairesis*] of these united ones."[28] The various terms used here give a general, but not a precise, sense of the divine unity, a generality also evidenced when Athenagoras wrote of the Father, Son, and Spirit "being united in power and distinct in rank."[29] He employed analogies such as "the rays of the sun" and "light from fire"[30] to describe the Spirit as the "effluence" of God, which "flows from and returns" to God,[31] analogies that speak less of any essential unity and more of a oneness based in and sustained through the Father's oneness.[32] That said, the overall sense is that the Logos is the inseparable and eternal Mind of the God "who is" and the Spirit is the same eternal God's Spirit.

Where Theophilos may diverge slightly from Justin's and Athenagoras's thinking concerning the Logos *endiathetos* and *prophorikos* is in the relation of his thinking to that of Stoicism. For in Theophilos's writings there are hints that his thinking may be nearer to that of Philo. It is not that Theophilos turned his back on Stoicism, even though it must be recognized that Theophilos was generally critical of

27. Athenagoras, *Plea*, 10.4.

28. Athenagoras, *Plea*, 12.3.

29. Athenagoras, *Plea*, 24.2.

30. Athenagoras, *Plea*, 10.4 and 24.2 respectively.

31. Athenagoras, *Plea*, 10.4.

32. Plotinus used similar analogies to illustrate his understanding of how everything emanates from the One. See Louth, *The origins of the Christian mystical* tradition, 39.

the philosophies of Hellenism. It is rather that Theophilos, whose background lay primarily in the world of Hellenistic Judaism, came close to Philo's idea, not common in Greek philosophy, that God is one who "*speaks*." Reflecting on the creation narrative of Genesis 1, Philo referred to creation as a result of God *speaking*. He wrote of the Creator as the one who produced the world by a "word."[33] In this regard Theophilos is not as explicit as Philo. Yet he did relate that the Logos had been expressed to effect the world's creation; and, in a passage that refers to the Genesis account of God saying, "Let there be light," and to God's "calling" the light "day" and the darkness "night," Theophilos referred to God's creative Logos as "the command of God."[34] If there is in Theophilos's thinking some sense that God created the universe by his speaking, by his Word, there is also then some sense there of God's effortless Lordship over matter, a sense that alludes to both God and his Logos being sovereignly distinct from and yet intimately concerned for all that was called and held in being as the sovereign God's "servant."

THEIST INDEED, WHO WORKED WITH AN APPLIED THEOLOGY

A number of these understandings of God were formed and shaped in the context of a Christian–Jewish debate, such as that between Justin and Trypho. Yet, for all that, there were implications for the wider Hellenistic audience before which Justin sought to make his defense that Christians were not guilty of the charge of atheism. Hence, Justin's describing the one God in whom Christians trusted and God's world of which everyone was an integral part. There could be no denying that the Logos was distinct from the

33. Philo, *On Flight*, 95.

34. Theophilos, *To Autolycus*, 2.13.

Father—for, as Justin held, the Logos was not as sunlight is to the sun, distinct "in name" only, but "numerically" distinct, as a fire kindled from a fire is distinct.[35] Yet the same Logos was God, the "second" God, the *deuteros theos*. The Logos was "second" and "God" in the sense of being "begotten from the Father, by God's power and will, but not by abscission, as if the Father's essence had been divided, or violently separated—for everything else, once partitioned and divided, is not the same . . . as it was beforehand."[36] The Logos was also "second" and "God" in the sense of being the Logos whom the Unbegotten begetter "established . . . in the beginning as the beginner of all things,"[37] as God's instrument of all creating.

When these various understandings of the God of the Christians were allowed to speak with one voice, they spoke of a Logos who is closely, personally related to God, and of a Logos *endiathetos* who then is the Logos *prophorikos*, one who "links" God in his very being (God *ad intra*) with God in his gracious extension (God *ad extra*).

There is, however, more than an academic argument here. For, alongside the implicit criticism here of the worship of the cult of the domestic *lararia*, of the temple, and of the imperial court—for that made is not to be worshipped—there is also the assertion that matter, as made and remade by God in and through the divine Logos, though not to be worshipped, was to be treated with the utmost moral seriousness. So, for example, in his discussion with the Jew Trypho, Justin pondered the need to practice fasting. Fasting he did not dismiss as an aspect of the Jewish law, no longer of significance in the Christian

35. Justin, *Dialogue with Trypho*, 128.4.

36. Justin, *Dialogue with Trypho*, 128.4.

37. Justin, *Dialogue with Trypho*, 126 and 129, quoting Proverbs 8:22.

dispensation. Nor did he commend fasting—as certain strands of Pythagorean philosophy and of Gnosticism did—as a means by which a soul, presently trapped in the material, temporal world, might extricate itself and begin its destined flight to the Alone.[38] Rather, Justin understood fasting as a spiritual act manifested in such very mundane and material acts as the freeing of the oppressed, the feeding the hungry, the clothing the naked, and the housing the homeless.[39] Though the world was not to be worshipped, it was to be taken seriously. Especially when marred, it was to be taken very seriously. Then, above all, as the anonymous writer to Diognetus observed, Christians, who "are poor . . . make many rich."[40]

The Apologists further evidenced an applied theism in their treatment of God's gracious actions in relation to the ancient people of Israel, of the incarnation and of the final judgement. Theophilos, the writer to Diognetus, and Justin treat God's mercy in these respective regards.

It was not out of ignorance, Theophilos maintained, that God asked Adam and Eve, once they had eaten of the fruit of the tree of knowledge, "where are you?" Rather, it was "because [God] was patient and gave [Adam] an occasion for repentance and confession."[41] Indeed, from beginning to end, from the setting Adam and Eve in the garden of Eden, to the calling them, and to the temporarily expelling them from the garden, Theophilos held, God acted providentially. Through the command not to eat of the tree of the knowledge of good and evil God was testing humanity's readiness to obey. Yet they disobeyed. Nevertheless, God did not forsake them. God continued to invite

38. Justin, *Dialogue with Trypho*, 80.

39. Justin, *Dialogue with Trypho*, 15, quoting Isaiah 58:1–12.

40. *To Diognetus*, 5.13.

41. Theophilos, *To Autolycus*, 2.26.

humanity's repentance and obedience. Indeed, through the punishment of banishment, God granted them the opportunity, in a set period of time, to make expiation for their sins and, after chastisement, to be recalled, following the resurrection and the final judgement, namely, at the end of the time of "temporary exclusion," to paradise, the second garden, the new "Eden."[42]

Not that God's concern for the world began and ended with these two figures. Cognizant that others would invent many, non-existent gods, Theophilos drew the attention of his readers to God causing it to be said "In the beginning God made the heaven and the earth."[43] Few other texts could make it clearer as to who made things, who and what was ordered, and so who rightly was to be worshipped. So, on reading these words from the book of Genesis, Theophilos held, attentive people might draw back and reflect upon creation and its harmonious order. Then they might discern from the order of heaven and earth the One who gave them their order, and so be turned from worshipping the many "non-existent" gods to the "truly existent" God, the Creator of all that is made. Indeed, Theophilos added, God not only gave humanity such a verbal warning lest it should worship anything made but also endued humanity with the capacity to read creation aright, that all might worship only the harmoniously ordering God. So Theophilos's God heaped grace upon grace. Not that even that was the end of God's manifest concern for the world of matter. For Theophilos further wrote of God's having given humanity the Law, then the prophets—"illiterate men and shepherds,"[44] whose obvious lack of education only underlined the fact that the wisdom that they spoke was not of human but divine origin, and

42. Theophilos, *To Autolycus*, 2.22–26.

43. Theophilos, *To Autolycus*, 2.10, quoting Genesis 1:1.

44. Theophilos, *To Autolycus*, 2.35.

so all the more meet to be heeded—and then the Gospels. Severally and together, these acts of mercy, enacted to draw people back to God, emphasized Theophilos's sense of God's concerned relationship for the world of matter, a relationship of patient engagement and of merciful judgement to effect renewal. An unconcerned God, a solitary God, would not have been so patient, so merciful.

In his *Letter to Diognetus*, the letter writer reflected upon the fact that in former times God had allowed humanity to be carried away by undisciplined impulses. Such "permissiveness" the letter writer attributed, not to a divine delight in or an approval of human sin,[45] but to the Master and Maker of the universe being long-suffering, "slow to anger, . . . alone good."[46] Such "tolerance" Diognetus's correspondent explained as an example of divine patience, an outcome of God's goodness. For in and through God's temporarily leaving humanity's unrighteousness unchecked, God was enabling sinful humanity to become conscious of its being "unworthy of life," of its incapacity in and by itself to enter the kingdom of God, and of its being capable of doing so only "by the power of God."[47] Only later in time did the "Ruler of all" send the "Designer and Maker of the universe"[48] to humanity, humanity only now aware both of its sinfulness and helplessness and of God's "goodness and power to save";[49] and only then did the One send the Other as a man to humanity, to save humanity "by persuasion and not compulsion. For compulsion is not God's way of working."[50] There is here not only a sense of God's care for

45. *To Diognetus*, 9.1.

46. *To Diognetus*, 8.8.

47. *To Diognetus*, 9.1.

48. *To Diognetus*, 7.2.

49. *To Diognetus*, 9.2.

50. *To Diognetus*, 7.4.

the world of matter but also of a divine self-accommodation to sinful humanity's state. Indeed, there is here a sense of God so acting for humanity, but only when humanity would be ready to benefit the most. No wonder then that this correspondent wrote that God did not send the Logos "as a human mind might assume, to rule by tyranny and fear and terror. . . . He sent him out of kindness and love."[51] In that sense, the incarnation, for this letter writer, was a *"kairos"* moment, an opportune time, a time particularly suited to humanity's condition. Once again, although in a different theological context, an Apologist evidenced here that sense of God being ever concerned for the world of matter, even, as in this particular case, for humanity in its very fragile, sinful creatureliness.

The same sense of divine patience in exercising judgement, which evidenced the Maker's deep and ongoing salvific concern for what God had made, appears in the Apologists's reflections on Christ's first and second coming. For there also there is that sense of a patient, extensive mercy and a delayed judgement. Perhaps this is most obvious in the writings of Justin.

Justin believed that people could not live a morally neutral life. People were either for or against the one and only God. They were either the "friends of God,"[52] whom God willed all to be, or the absolute antithesis of "friends of God," God's enemies, whose sentence ultimately was condemnation. When, however, prior to the final sentencing, it was found that a person was an enemy of God, God's mercy, Justin maintained, was not then immediately ended. For while judgement was then made, a final sentencing was yet mercifully not immediately made, in order that

51. *To Diognetus*, 7.3–4.

52. Justin, *Dialogue with Trypho*, 28 and *Dialogue with Trypho*, 139.

such individuals might still have time to acknowledge the error of their ways, repent, and be spared condemnation. Indeed, to prompt the "enemies of God" to see the error of their ways, to turn from their inimical, ungodly acts and to live, Justin often reminded his audience of the terrible final state that was to be the inevitable fate of all who permanently separated themselves from the Maker and Judge of all. Indeed, at times Justin seems almost to *threaten* his non-Christian audience with the horrors of eternal punishment in order that, even at the eleventh hour, they might thereby be persuaded to turn from their errant ways and turn to the one, true God.[53]

Interestingly, that mercy which underlay the delay in implementing any final sentencing was not viewed as somehow limited nor as impaired by the use of the *threat* of final condemnation as an instrument of persuasion. The threat might even have rendered God's mercy a more obvious and robust mercy. For ever-hardening hearts often needed that more robust mercy. Indeed, Justin's thinking, especially when viewed within the context of his dialogue with the Jew Trypho, appears not to be so very different from that of the Jew Philo, who had argued that it was better to worship God out of fear than not to worship God at all, even if it might be better to worship God for hope of reward, and yet better still to worship God out of love.[54] The motives might have been of an ascending order of purity and praiseworthiness; yet all were acceptable. Nor was a Justin's God so rendered an irascible God. For the eternal punishment was seen, not

53. See Justin, *Apology*, 1.12; 1.52 and Justin, *Dialogue with Trypho*, 28. See also *To Diognetus*, 10.7–8 with its contrasting the "apparent death here below" with "the real death kept for those who are condemned to the eternal fires."

54. Philo, *On Abraham*, 128–130. See Louth, *The Origins of the Christians Mystical Tradition*, 23–24.

as that willed by an angry, irritated God whose mercy eventually had been exhausted but as the inevitable future of all who separated themselves from God in their concentrating upon themselves. Once again, the impropriety of worshipping matter, or self, and the propriety of knowing that God, the Maker of all, is concerned for each and all are prevalent in the Apologists's denial that they were "atheists."

As with the responses to the other accusations levelled against the mid-to-late second-century Christians, so with the defense against the accusation of Christians being atheists, the arguments here extend beyond theoretical arguments. The writer of the *Letter to Diognetus*, for example, was in keeping with the spirit of the other Apologists when he held before his reader, and any others who might have been looking over his letter reader's shoulder, the possibility of accepting his arguments. For a Christian reader of his letter, accepting his arguments meant, among other things, finding arguments that they might marshal in discussions with their non-Christian neighbors; and for non-Christian neighbors, accepting these arguments meant their abandoning atheism and its ways, and exchanging the worship of the gods of the cults for that of the one and only God. The letter writer's challenge to the Greco-Roman world was to cease falsely accusing Christians of being "atheists" and to begin to stand with them in their monotheism. Indeed, playing with words, the letter writer invited his readers to forsake the ways and worship of the gods of the empire, to become "god" to the needy by providing the needy with what they in their need had previously received from the one and only ever-generous God, and, rather than charging Christians with atheism, to admire those so wrongly charged and now punished for "their refusal to deny God."[55] Like other Apologists, this letter writer wished, above all,

55. *To Diognetus*, 10.7.

that those whom he viewed as the true atheists might become one of those falsely accused of being atheists.

QUESTIONS FOR REFLECTION
AND DISCUSSION

1. When thinking about the act of creation, the Apologists worked, not with the idea of creating the cosmos from nothing, but with that of God fashioning pre-existent matter, giving it shape and order. Does allowing the "existence" of pre-existent, unorganized matter that is then shaped into the ordered world of matter undermine belief in both the oneness and the sovereignty of God? In other words, if matter has *always existed* in some form or other does this undermine monotheism?

2. How justifiable is it to put, if not the fear of God, the Judge of all, at least that of eternal punishment into people in order to effect their repentance, their holiness of living now, and their being granted life eternal hereafter?

3. Is a "final judgement" at odds with God's enduring mercy?

4. The Apologists held that the Creator God made and moves the world. In a sense they viewed the world sacramentally. In what ways should so viewing the world alter contemporary ways of looking upon our fellow creatures, human and non-human?

5. In seeking to explain the relationship of God and the Word Justin employed both scriptural and philosophical vocabulary and both domestic and celestial imagery. Is there is a limit to what vocabulary and which images may be used to describe God? If not, why not? And, if so, what is it, and why?

6

THYESTEAN BANQUETS AND OEDIPEAN INTERCOURSE

SOMEHOW PEOPLE HAD HEARD that, in some of their services, Christians consumed a man's body and blood. Somehow they also had learned that Christians were encouraged to love one another, a love expressed especially by the promiscuous sharing of a kiss. On hearing that, people more hostile to Christianity began to spread rumors. Like Thyestes, who, at a feast hosted by his embittered brother Atreus, was served and then fed on the flesh of one of his own children, Christians, some of the wider public rumored, also engaged in Thyestean feasts; and like Oedipus who, on ascending to the throne of Thebes, not knowing that Jocasta was his mother, married Jocasta, who then bore him two sons and two daughters, Christians, the same people put abroad, participated in Oedipean intercourse.[1] In the face of such

1. See, for example, Athenagoras, *Plea*. 3.1; Justin, *Apology*, 2.3.

damaging rumors the Apologists not surprisingly sought to demonstrate how false these rumors were; and they sought to do so, perhaps more obviously here than when they attempted to address other charges levelled against them, with a certain commonality of arguments.

This commonality is evidenced, for example, in the Apologists's common denial that there was any substance whatsoever to the rumors. It is to be seen in their maintaining that merely being *accused* of being a "Christian"—one who allegedly attended Thyestean feasts or engaged in Oedipean intercourse—could not justify punishment, even as an individual's simply being *accused* of being a "bandit," without any attempt whatsoever to substantiate such an accusation, was insufficient grounds for imposing a guilty sentence.[2] In no walk of life, the Apologists insisted, was an uninvestigated accusation legitimate grounds for a verdict of "guilty."

This commonality of arguments is further to be found in the Christians's insistence, to which we shall return, that, given the eternal terrors that Christians believed would be meted out upon sinners at the final judgement by God, even if only to avoid such dire, eternal punishments, Christians would rigorously resist any involvement in such sinful acts as cannibalism and incest.

Such arguments the Apologists shared. They did, however, put forward other, more individual ones.

THYESTEAN FEASTS

Justin, for example, in his attempt to scotch what, to his mind, were baseless rumors concerning Christian involvement in Thyestean feasts, questioned aspects of the

See also Eusebius , *Ecclesiastical History*, 5.1.14.

2. See Tatian, *Address*, 27.1; Justin, *Apology*, 1.68; Athenagoras, *Plea*, 3.1; 4; Eusebius, *Ecclesiastical History*, 4.9.

procedure employed by those whom he considered the ru-
mor-mongers. Some of the informants used in the attempt
to give substance to the rumored immorality, Justin pointed
out, were slaves. Yet slaves, he insisted, should not have been
so used. For, as he was at pains to remind his readers, slaves,
by their very servile status, were excluded from having a
role in the empire's formal and public life, and so, by extension, slaves should also have been denied any role in the investigating any charges brought against Christians. To this
warning against procedural malpractice Justin then added
a further warning against anyone naïvely or misguidedly
assuming that the words of slaves were always trustworthy.
He directed his readers's attention to the fact that some of
the slaves who had said that their Christian masters had
engaged in such immorality were but children while others
were weak women, two groups then commonly held not to
be reliable and trustworthy witnesses. He highlighted the
possibility that some of the slaves, upon whose words those
who had brought charges against Christians relied, were
prejudiced against their Christian owners and masters; and
prejudiced words, he insisted, did not make fair trials. Further, he noted, some of these slaves upon whose testimony
those hostile to Christianity relied were victims of torture,
torture sometimes inflicted by torturers acting under the
prompting of wicked demons;[3] and any testimony elicited
under torture, especially demonically driven torture, made
a mockery of justice's proper demand for the whole truth.
So, even if and when charges levelled against Christians
were investigated, these investigations, Justin concluded,
often fell far short of what justice required.

3. See also *The Letter of the Churches of Lyons and Vienne*, 14,
where there is reference to certain pagan slaves who, "enslaved by Sa-
tan and terrified of the tortures which they saw the faithful suffering,
at the soldiers' instigation falsely accused the Christians of Oedipean
marriages and being diners in the manner of Thyestes."

Justin then switched tack. Why, he teasingly wondered, if, as alleged by some slaves, Christians were cannibals, would Christians welcome death, in particular a premature martyr's death, when death meant the putting to an end the very "Thyestean feast" in which Christians allegedly took such pleasure? Or why, if Christians were cannibals, rather than welcoming an early death, and so an untimely end to their cannibalism, did they not rather readily admit their cannibalistic practices, publicly profess that they deemed these practices to be "good," and maintain that, like those others who without hindrance or challenge poured bloody libations before the statue of Saturn, they too were simply engaging in the "mysteries of Saturn"?[4]

In this regard Theophilos argued to the same end as Justin had. Yet, the shape of his argument often was different. Unlike Justin, he avoided even a light-hearted teasing of his opponents. Equally, he resisted employing such speculative questions as "if Christians so delighted in Thyestean feasts, why were they so ready to put an end to that delight by being so ready to accept an end to this life?" Rather, Theophilos stated his beliefs confidently and unequivocally. If charges of cannibalism were to be brought against anyone, should they not, he asked, rightly be levelled against, not Christians, but such people as Zeno, Diogenes, and Cleanthes?[5] For it was *they* and not Christians, he maintained, who, in their books, had commended cannibalism. Should not such charges, Theophilos further asked, be brought against the gods of the Greek myths? For it was *they* who were honored for having been the first to eat human flesh. Christians, he implied, who neither taught nor practiced cannibalism, were instruments of godliness. In contrast, the followers of the writings of Zeno and the like, and the devotees of the gods of the Greek myths,

4. Justin, *Apology*, 2.12.

5. Theophilos, *To Autolycus*, 3.5.

he insisted, were vehicles of ungodliness. With hyperbolic horror Theophilos concluded, "O, the godless teaching of those who . . . advocate such activity! O, the impiety and godlessness! . . . Those who have propounded such teachings have completely filled the world with impiety!"[6]

Against the same charge Athenagoras advanced a different defense. That human flesh had been eaten, Athenagoras argued, presupposes that a human being had previously been killed. Yet there was no evidence, he continued, of people having been killed in Christian households. Not even the slaves in the various Christian households—whose witness Athenagoras, in contrast with Justin's judgement, implied could be trusted, and from whom nothing could be hidden or remain hidden—had seen Christians acquiescing with, let alone taking part in, the killing of a person, upon whose flesh they might subsequently have feasted. Indeed, Athenagoras continued, there was not and nor could there be any such evidence for the simple reason that Christians were wholly opposed to murder in any context. So they shunned contests in which gladiators fought amongst themselves, seeking to kill their opponents, or in which people risked their lives when fighting against wild animals. Further, they resisted exposure to the pollution and the contaminating defilement that came of witnessing the killing of another human being.[7] Athenagoras's argument was not dissimilar from Theophilos's: Christians, Athenagoras maintained, attended neither gladiatorial shows, "lest [they] should become participants and accomplices in murder,"[8] nor plays, for fear of hearing of Thyestean feasts and so finding their ears and eyes defiled. Christians, Athenagoras continued, further evidenced their opposition

6. Theophilos, *To Autolycus*, 3.5.

7. Athenagoras, *Plea*, 35.4–5.

8. Theophilos, *To Autolycus*, 3.15.

to murder in their also counting as murderers those who practiced abortion or who exposed unwanted children.[9] In short, if Christians, a Theophilos and an Athenagoras argued, would not tolerate the killing of anyone—whether in real life, in an amphitheater or in a peri-natal context, or in fiction, in a play at the theater—how much less would they kill and then feast on a fellow human being?

If anyone was to be found guilty of feeding on human flesh, Athenagoras chided, it was the city's pimps and those who used prostitutes, male or female. For they were "like fish, . . . [swallowing] up whoever [came] their way, the stronger consuming the weaker."[10] They, not the Christians who prayed for the emperor and who kept the law, insofar as it was consonant with God's commandments,[11] were those who violated the ancient laws of justice. They, not the Christians, were those who should stand charged with the crime of cannibalism, a crime made even more heinous in that they "consumed" the weakest and the most vulnerable in society.

Interestingly, although the accusation that Christians participated in Thyestean feasts seems to have been based on a misrepresentation of the Eucharist, most of the mid-to-late second-century Apologists gave no description of

9. On abortion see Athenagoras, *Plea*, 35.6 where the fetus is described as "a living being and, for that reason, an object of God's concern," and, more widely, in the Christian tradition, *Didache*, 2.2; *Letter of Barnabas*, 19.5, and, in Jewish tradition, Philo, *On Special Laws*, 3.108–115; Josephus, *Against Apion*, 2.202. On exposing unwanted children see Athenagoras, *Plea*, 35.6 and Justin, *Apology*, 1.27.

10. Athenagoras, *Plea*, 34.3.

11. See Justin, *Apology*, 2.12, where Christians are portrayed as being allies and helpers of the emperor in promoting all godly peace, and Justin, *Apology*, 1.7; 1.68, where Christians are pictured as pleading with the imperial rulers to do only what is pleasing to God. See also Tatian, *Address*, 4.1: "only God is to be feared."

the Eucharist, that any misrepresentation of it might be corrected. Not, in some sense, that that is surprising. For, at that time, even catechumens, until admitted into the church, were shielded from the full details of an eucharistic celebration. That may explain why words very reminiscent of the eucharistic prayer of general thanksgiving found in the *Apostolic Constitutions*,[12] and which, as a bishop, Theophilos in all likelihood would have often recited, were included by Theophilos in his response to Autolycus, not to describe, even in general terms, the very rite that erroneously had given rise to the rumors and charges of cannibalism, but to praise God as the Creator.[13]

Another reason for generally not including a description of the Eucharist in an *Apology* may be that the including any description could have been counter-productive. Certainly, that may well have been the case when Justin described it. In his *Dialogue with Trypho* Justin was content to admit that Christians, "in every place [offered] sacrifices to [God], namely, the bread of the eucharist and also the cup of the eucharist."[14] Had Justin limited his description to such, his language may have helped the case of his Christian contemporaries who had been accused of being cannibals. Mention of "bread" and of a "cup" made no Christian a hostage to fortune; and it would have been but an echo of what Pliny had written to Trajan when Pliny reported to Trajan that Christians assembling on a fixed day of the week, when, amongst other things, they took "food, *but ordinary and harmless food.*[15] Indeed, it implicitly suggested that Christians did not engage in cannibalistic

12. Theophilos, *To Autolycus*, 1.6–7. See also *Apostolic Constitutions*, 7.34–35.

13. Justin, *Dialogue with Trypho*, 47.

14. Justin, *Dialogue with Trypho*, 41.

15. Pliny, *Letters*, 10.96.7. The italics are mine.

rites when celebrating the Eucharist. In his First *Apology*, however, Justin went beyond mentioning the bread and the cup. There he wrote of the eucharistic community's prayers, the shared kiss of peace, the blessing of bread and of wine mixed with water, and the receiving those blessed elements, having been taught that these elements were "the flesh and the blood of that Jesus who was made flesh."[16] Justin's description was not defensive, but confidently open. Yet Justin's open confidence in admitting that Christians consumed "the flesh and the blood of that Jesus" may, in all probability, only have further strengthened the thinking of Christianity's critics and furthered the spreading of rumors that Christians were indeed cannibals who partook in Thyestean-like, or even Thyestean feasts.

OEDIPEAN INTERCOURSE

Had the rumors concerning Christians engaging in shameless intercourse with women been true, Christians, Justin suggested, could have addressed the matter by admitting that they simply were "imitating Jupiter and the other gods." They could have brought forward "as [their] apology the writings of Epicurus and the poets."[17] However, these rumors, the Apologists severally asserted, were not true; and so, they continued, Christians could not, without lying, make such an admission or apology. Rather, being the followers of the Truth, they had to tell the truth. So Aristides wrote, Christian wives truly were "as pure as virgins, [Christian] daughters [were] . . . modest, and Christian men abstained from both all unlawful marriage and from all iniquity."[18]

16. Justin, *Apology*, 1.66.

17. Justin, *Apology*, 2.12.

18. Aristides, *Apology*, 15 and Aristides, *Apology*, 17.2. Through the phrase "from all iniquity," both passages possibly allude to

Other Apologists echoed Aristides's assertions. Christians, Athenagoras observed, often remained single. For virginity was seen as bringing a person "closer to God."[19] If they did marry, they then might engage in sexual intercourse, yet "not for any licentious purpose,"[20] something that not even wild irrational animals did,[21] but, as Justin and Athenagoras maintained, "only in . . . order to raise children."[22] More generally, Diognetus's correspondent succinctly noted that married Christians "share their board with others, but not their bed."[23] Indeed, the strict sexual morality that lay behind the Apologists's insistence on monogamy both led Justin and Theophilos, who preferred the dominical teaching reported in Matthew 19:9 to that in Mark 10:11, to forbid divorce in all cases save those in which unfaithfulness on the part of one of the married couple had occurred, and prompted

---

Romans 1:26 with its reference to God giving up those who were unfaithful to the Creator of all "to impurity, to the degrading of their bodies amongst themselves." See also Justin, *Apology*, 2.12, where, in resisting charges of immorality brought against Christians, Justin also listed sodomy alongside men's "shameless intercourse with women."

19. Athenagoras, *Plea*, 33.2–3. See also Justin, *Apology*, 1.15 where, quoting Matthew 19:12, Justin celebrated those Christian men and women who, Christ's disciples from childhood, are still "pure" at the age of sixty or seventy years, and all "for the sake of the kingdom of heaven."

20. Athenagoras, *Plea*, 3.1.

21. See such psalms as Psalm 49:12,20 and Psalm 73:21, and such passages as 2 Peter 2:12 and Jude 10, where a person without understanding is likened to a beast. If there is an allusion by Athenagoras to such scriptural texts here, there is also the thought here that, if a wild beast will not engage in sexual licentiousness, all the less should a rational human.

22. Justin, *Apology*, 1.15. Athenagoras, *Plea*, 33.1–2. See also Tatian, *Address*, 33.2 where Christian wives are described as "chaste."

23. *To Diognetus* 5.7.

Athenagoras to forbid divorce in every case.[24] Interestingly, the teaching on divorce of each of these several Apologists stands in marked contrast with the late second-century custom, developed on the back of the *Lex Papia Poppaea* of AD 9, of allowing divorce and then of requiring divorced women between the ages of twenty and fifty years to remarry within a few years of any divorce, in order that further legitimate child citizens might be born.

Adultery and the coveting of another man's wife Athenagoras, in common with other Apologists's reading of the Decalogue, condemned. Indeed, he was not prepared to condone a second marriage, even when a person's spouse from a first marriage had died. "Gilded adultery"[25] was what he titled a second marriage. That noted, his thinking here, it must be admitted, was not out of keeping with his prioritizing the practices of men and women "growing old unmarried in the hope of being united more closely with God" over marriage, even when sexual intercourse or, as Athenagoras termed it, "the indulgence of our lust," was limited to the confines of marriage, and its end to procreation. In this Athenagoras exceeded in rigor Justin's and Theophilos's thinking that, while someone marrying a divorced person did render that person a partner in adultery,[26] a second marriage on the death of a spouse, though permissible, was not to be encouraged.[27]

24. Athenagoras, *Plea*, 33.5. See also Justin, *Apology*, 2.2; Theophilos, *To Autolycus*, 3.13.

25. Athenagoras, *Plea*, 33.4. See also Athenagoras, *Plea*, 33.2–3.

26. Justin, *Apology*, 1.15. Theophilos, *To Autolycus*, 3.13. See also Matthew 5:32.

27. Justin, *Apology*, 1.29. See also Theophilos, *To Autolycus*, 2.28, where, alluding to Genesis 2:24, marriage is seen as an ancient and honourable estate, ordained by God. Tatian, however, after the martyrdom of his teacher Justin, is recorded by Irenaeus, in *Against the Heresies*, 1.28.1, as having separated himself from the church and

Given such thinking, Athenagoras was therefore more than content to insist that Christians did not and would not commit adultery, even in thought. For, he asserted, they lived in accordance with the teaching of Matthew's Jesus, mindful that even to look lustfully on a woman was already to have committed "adultery in one's heart."[28] Therefore, he stressed, the kiss shared at the Eucharist was not a kiss given or received in the pursuit of pleasure, a pursuit that immediately would have placed the giver of the kiss and its receiver "outside eternal life."[29] Rather, that kiss was a *single* kiss, a single kiss *of peace*, shared between fellow Christians, between "brother" and "sister" and "father" and "mother." These were familial titles, Athenagoras continued, that were based, not in any *physical kinship*—so making this kiss very different from any kiss that may have been shared between an Oedipus and a Jocasta—but based upon the age of and the honor properly due to each Christian. So, for example, a "father" was so titled because of his venerable age and his widely recognized dignity. The kiss shared at the Eucharist was, therefore, shared, not according to the flesh, but "*in God.*" It was a kiss, or, more accurately, a "reverential greeting."[30] The kiss given at the Eucharist consequently neither violated the bodies of any nor sullied the "spiritual" kinship of Christian with Christian or of Christian with God. In brief, for Athenagoras, the kiss of the Eucharist was then evidence, not of

---

then composed his own particular type of doctrine, one corollary of which was that "he declared that marriage was nothing else than corruption and fornication."

28. Athenagoras, *Plea*, 32.2. See also Matthew 5:28; Justin, *Apology*, 1.15.

29. Athenagoras, *Plea*, 32.5.

30. Athenagoras, *Plea*, 32.6. This thinking reflects that found in, for example, Romans 16:16; 1 Corinthians 16:20; 2 Corinthians 13:12; 1 Thessalonians 5:26 and 1 Peter 5:14.

sexual immorality, but of the church's reconciled unity in the one true and all holy God.[31]

Given then that, amongst Christians, it was generally maintained both that sexual intercourse was to be limited to that between husband and wife, and then only for the begetting of children, and that children were to be shown how valuable they were in and through their being given a "reverential greeting" at the Eucharist, it is understandable that people like Justin agreed with but added to the assertion of the writer to Diognetus that Christians did not expose their children. This Justin did by drawing the attention of his readers to the fact that Christians not only did not expose their children but actually rescued unwanted infants whom others had exposed to die. In part they did this, he insisted, out of a concern to obey the sixth commandment, not to murder. In part they also did this, he continued, for the sake both of the providers and the purchasers of the services of child prostitutes and of the state. For, firstly, Christians were concerned lest pimps might "rescue" exposed infants, not for wholesome reasons, but in order to augment the number of child prostitutes. Interestingly, the concern of Christians here, Justin reported, was not only for innocent children, important as that was. Their concern was also for any providers and purchasers of the services of child prostitutes, providers and purchasers who, by so increasing the number of child prostitutes and thus making "godless, infamous and impure intercourse" yet more widely available,[32] might

31. See also Cyril of Jerusalem, *Catecheses*, 23.3, where readers are advised to "think not that [the kiss of peace] ranks with those given in public by common friends . . . This kiss blends souls one with another, and solicits from them entire forgiveness. Therefore this kiss is the sign that our souls are mingled together and have banished all remembrance of wrong. The kiss therefore is reconciliation, and for that reason is holy."

32. Justin, *Apology*, 1.27.

the more readily so inflict upon themselves spiritual harm. Secondly, the Christians were especially fearful lest those parents who had exposed their offspring should then heap sin upon sin. For they were anxious lest those who formerly had sinned in exposing their unwanted children and later went in search of sexual gratification might unknowingly then procure the services of their very own children, now prostitutes, and find themselves guilty of the very charges that they improperly levelled against Christians. The use here by Justin of the clause "having intercourse with their own child" very much suggests that an allusion to Jocasta's intercourse with her very own child Oedipus is intended to be heard. To all intents and purposes Justin here seems to be saying to those who accused Christians of having engaged in Oedipean intercourse: Let those who have ears to hear, hear. Thirdly, the Apologists were anxious lest the state, which then taxed prostitution, should grow ever more prosperous at the expense of the very ones whom, in their vulnerability, it should especially cherish, and not exploit.

Further, given that Christians held that even looking lustfully upon a woman constituted adultery, it is understandable that Apologists such as Tatian and Theophilos, as part of their defense of Christians against the charges of involvement in Oedipean intercourse, drew the attention of their accusers to the fact that Christians refused both to gaze upon even statues of the female form and to attend theaters. On moral, rather than aesthetic grounds, they distanced themselves from their neighbors who admired the statues of, for example, a one-time prostitute or a wanton or a singer of lewd songs or an adulteress. Not Christians but those who allowed their gaze to linger upon these naked female forms, Tatian implied, were the people who were guilty of sexual immorality.[33] Change the statue for a *drama-*

33. Tatian, *Address*, 33–34.

tis persona and the same argument was marshalled. For in the theater actors donned theatrical masks and, even in the presence of children, the most impressionable members of society, and so the most in need of protection, played roles as varied as that of an adulterer or a teacher of perverts, so packaging immorality both poetically and persuasively. It was not Christians, but the theater audiences who, in and through their plaudits, sanctioned such immoral behavior and unacceptable teaching.

Theophilos similarly reflected on why, for moral reasons, Christians absented themselves from theaters. It was bad enough, he argued, that an actor played the part of an adulterer. It was worse that an actor's portrayal of adulterous behavior could, and often did, weaken a theater-goer's resolve to remain sexually chaste. For, as in life generally, so in the theater in particular, human beings could and often did influence fellow human beings, and not always for the better. That potential for influencing people not for the better was, however, the greater, Theophilos argued, when the *dramatis persona* portrayed on the stage as an adulterer was one of the deities of the Greek tragedies and when the portrayal was well-received. For a deity, by definition, was one who should be imitated by a human being; and, all the more likely was the behavior of such an adulterous deity to be imitated by a human being when the deity's behavior, despite the behavior being inglorious, was "proclaimed euphoniously" by actors whose very aim was to be so plausible that they might win "honors and prizes" from audiences and critics alike.[34] Each and all, play and performers and theater-going public alike, to Theophilos's mind, were therefore, iniquitously engaged not simply in condoning and normalizing but in promoting such godlessness; and in such Christians would have no part.

34. Theophilos, *To Autolycus*, 3.15.

The same sense of theaters promoting immorality probably may be found in Tatian's writing. Theater-going, Tatian certainly asserted, was "of no benefit."[35] If, however, note is then taken of Tatian's belief that the human soul, ignorant of the truth, "inclines towards matter and dies,"[36] theater-going, especially if audiences ignored the danger inherent in attending to actors skillfully inhabiting the roles of gods behaving immorally, would, to Tatian's way of thinking, in fact be worse than "of no benefit." It would be detrimental to beneficial living. For it would inflict actual moral harm, deepening a person's ignorance of true and holy living, and heightening moral turpitude.

When all these arguments and descriptions of the lives that Christians lived, rather than were rumored to live, were noted, it was clear, the Apologists suggested, how improper was the charge that Christians engaged in Oedipean intercourse.

If the mid-to-late second-century Christians were, in any sense of the word, "guilty" of the charge of being promiscuous, they were guilty only in relation to their showing an indiscriminate, generous love, especially to the most needy. Christians, the Apologists maintained, were people who loved one another as God had first loved them.[37] Echoing the Pauline injunction,[38] they were to bless even those who persecuted them.[39] They were to be long-suffering to all, even as God "had been, who caused the sun to rise on both the good and the evil, and the rain to fall on both the just and the unjust."[40] So they shared their food with all.

35. Tatian, *Address*, 24.1.

36. Tatian, *Address*, 13.2.

37. *To Diognetus*, 10.4. See also 1 John 4:19.

38. Romans 12:14.

39. *To Diognetus*, 5.15.

40. Athenagoras, *Plea*, 11.2. See also Matthew 5:44–45.

Fasting, they gave to the poor either the food not eaten or the money not spent on buying food, so acting in stark contrast with wider society, which was unequal and uncaring to the extent that, in it, a poor, hungry man could feel so abandoned that he might seek to earn money by selling himself to be a gladiator's victim in the amphitheater.[41] At the end of the Eucharist, the consecrated elements having been consumed, Christians took a collection, freely made, then to be distributed to, "in a word, all in need."[42] As already noted, they rescued unwanted children, exposed by ungodly parents. They commended hosting the homeless in their own homes and clothing the naked stranger.[43] They returned, not evil for evil, but employed a godly patience, blessing those who reviled them, their patience not forcing—for compulsion was not God's way, and so was not to be the way of those who would be godly[44]—but generously offering any who cursed them time to repent and amend their ways. If one corollary of God having made someone or something was that they should not be worshipped, another clearly was that they were to be tended with care, respected for being God-made.

Care for people extended beyond individual acts of kindness, It included ensuring, insofar as Christians could, that social justice was pursued. So, on the wider stage, Christians paid their taxes, prayed that right judgements in all matters might be made by the emperor and those others in high office, and supported the promotion of a godly peace and justice.[45] They were "in the world

41. Tatian, *Address*, 23.1.

42. Justin, *Apology*, 1.67.

43. Justin, *Dialogue with Trypho*, 15. See also Matthew 25:43.

44. *To Diognetus*, 7.4.

45. Justin, *Apology*, 1.12 See also Tatian, *Address*, 4.1.

what the soul was in the body,"[46] guarding the body politic from injurious passions and promoting its continuing health. They were "god" to the needy, giving of what God had freely given them.[47] They were to be as God's creative Word was to the world. For, as God's Word brought ordered creation from unformed, disorderly, pre-existent matter, so Christians, servants of God's Word, were to be God's agents bringing order to the confused world of second-century Rome.[48] In short, in the mid-to-late second century, Christians were promiscuous, but not at all in the manner suggested in the rumors falsely alleging that Christians engaged in Oedipean intercourse.

Of equal importance to the Apologists's denial that, in the past, Christians had engaged in Oedipean intercourse was their confident assertion that neither in the future would Christians ever engage in such. Christians neither had been guilty of sexual immorality, nor would they ever be. For Christians, as Aristides and Justin noted, had been "illuminated," a synonym for "baptized."[49] They had been called to live each day in the light of the Truth set before them. For them, in contrast with members of the various gnostic groupings, the knowledge with which they had been illuminated was not a knowledge comprised of certain truths, *information*, to be used to effect the human soul's release from the material and temporal world to its immaterial and atemporal home in an "alien" god. Rather, the knowledge that had been revealed to them was concerned with the living life here and now, especially when at its darkest. So Aristides, for example, recorded that as Jesus, when being crucified, prayed that his persecutors might be

46. *To Diognetus*, 6.1. See also Philo, *Embassy*, 1.3–4.

47. *To Diognetus*, 10.6.

48. Tatian, *Address*, 5.3.

49. Aristides, *Apology*, 17; Justin, *Apology*, 1.61.

forgiven, for "they [knew] not what they [were] doing,"[50] so Christians, those illumined, were also to pray for their persecutors, for those who were as "destitute of knowledge"[51] as Christ's persecutors, praying that those who did not know what they were doing might eventually turn from their errors. In short, Christians had been illuminated, baptized into the life of the dying Christ, made new in Christ. Even *in extremis* they had knowingly dedicated themselves to God.[52] Consequently, neither in the past, nor in the present, nor in the future had or would Christians follow either man-made opinions or adhere to the commonly agreed but also often contradictory traditions of this town or that state, or own or imitate the immoral lives of the gods of the many and various cults of the empire.

Setting aside mere human opinion, the customs and consensus of cities, and the inventions of the cults, Christians continued to seek to live in the light of God's revealed truth. So they sought to obey the Decalogue, the divine law properly to be kept by, not only Christians and the few other righteous in the world, but "the whole world."[53] Hence their observing its commandments not to commit adultery and murder. They also followed the teaching of Jesus, as, for example, reflected in the Gospel of Matthew's teaching concerning sexual chastity. They continually encouraged one another to speak and act as Jesus did, especially as and when he was faced with false charges and unjust condemnation.

The touchstone for Christian behavior, as in the past, so in the future, therefore, was the one God, the only Judge of all. This point, that God was the Judge of all, played a very significant part in the Apologists's arguments. For it alluded

50. Luke 23:24

51. Aristides, *Address*, 17.

52. See Justin, *Apology*, 1.61.

53. Theophilos, *To Autolycus*, 3.9.

to the fact that the mid-to-late second-century Apologists believed that all people then lived in the end-time and that how they lived in the end-time had consequences.

One particular consequence of living, not as God would, but in accordance with the traditions and customs of the mid-to-late second-century imperial cults and games and theaters, the Apologists commonly believed, would ultimately be a person's suffering an everlasting punishment "in the realms of fire."[54] Nor could this consequence be avoided. For no one, the Apologists asserted, could legitimately plead ignorance or avoid detection. For, in regard to the former, anyone could and should read the Scriptures and attend to "the doctrines which [Christians held], doctrines which were not the result of human conjecture but had been ordained and taught by God"[55]; and, in regard to the latter, all should acknowledge "that God knows what every individual thinks and says both by night and by day, and that [God], who is totally light, sees also what is in [people's] hearts."[56] So, Christians would, as all others should, avoid doing evil lest they should "deliver [themselves] up to the great Judge to be punished."[57] If for no other reason than to avoid the eternal fire of the end-time, Christians, the Apologists argued, in the past had abstained and in the future would continue to abstain from Thyestean feasts and Oedipean intercourse.

---

54. Athenagoras, *Plea*, 31.3. See also *To Diognetus*, 10.7–8 where persecution and any ensuing death are titled, respectively, the "transitory fire" and "the apparent death here below," in contrast with the eternal fires of the final judgement.

55. Athenagoras, *Plea*, 11.1.

56. Athenagoras, *Plea*, 31.3.

57. Athenagoras, *Plea*, 31.3. See also *To Diognetus*, 10.7; Justin, *Apology*, 1.12.

A MISSIONARY APOLOGY

As elsewhere, so here, a central thrust of the Apologists's writing was the defense of Christians against the unjustified charges of their critics. Yet equally, as elsewhere, so here, a significant concern of the Apologists was their engaging with God's missional purpose. For, for example, in asserting that Christians did not engage in such ungodly acts as murder, the Apologists implicitly were criticizing those in wider mid-to-late second-century society who murdered others in exposing infants, or sanctioned murder through attending gladiatorial shows; and in adhering to the scriptural injunctions not to commit adultery, either in thought or deed, Christians implicitly judged those who committed adultery through, for example, delighting in the sexual antics of the gods of Greek plays and poems or participating in the riotous rituals of such cults as that of Bacchus.

That, however, was not the sum of the matter. For the Apologists also were implicitly inviting their critics and oppressors to repent of their ungodly ways and so avoid the final eternal punishment that was to be the lot of all the ungodly. Christians certainly were not minded to force God's way upon others. For, as the letter writer to Diognetus maintained, God willed to save humanity "by persuasion and not by compulsion,"[58] and, as Justin held, "the Almighty God is kind and merciful to all."[59] Christians were rather to be "kind and merciful as [their] heavenly Father [was],"[60] that their God-like ways, rather than, as was often the case, inciting antagonism towards the godly, might attract the

58. *To Diognetus*, 7.4.

59. Justin, *Dialogue with Trypho*, 96, quoting Matthew 5:45 concerning God's causing the sun to rise and the rain to fall on the ungrateful and on the righteous.

60. Justin, *Dialogue with Trypho*, 96, quoting Luke 6:35.

ungodly to God.[61] Christians, however, were, at one and the same time, also to alert their audiences to the righteous but still merciful ways of the Judge of all. Diognetus's correspondent was not exceptional amongst the Apologists. He wrote of "the eternal fires which will punish to the end those who are handed over to them";[62] and he did so in the hope of persuading Diognetus and any other reader of his letter to repent of their former ungodly ways and turn, before it was too late, to the God of Christianity.

Yet, maybe more obviously than did the other Apologists, Diognetus's correspondent also qualified such an eschatological argument with one that relied less on prompting human fear and more on appreciating God's ongoing merciful goodness as that which shaped the missional dimension of his apology. And that qualification's more obvious presence in the *Letter to Diognetus* cannot easily be explained simply by suggesting that, in comparison with the writings of the other mid-to-late second-century Apologists, the correspondence with Diognetus was less an apology, with a defensive edge, and more a letter gently seeking to inform its recipient's "accurate and careful investigation of [the religion of Christians]."[63]

Towards the end of the letter, the letter writer encouraged Diognetus to love God who first had loved Diognetus. He then added, "and when you love [God], you will be an imitator of [God's] goodness."[64] If and when Diognetus then were to begin to love God, that imitating of God's goodness would be seen, for example, in Diognetus's abstaining from lording it over his neighbor and in his making provision for the needy out of his own abundance. It would, however,

61. See Justin, *Apology*, 2.4.

62. *To Diognetus*, 10.7.

63. *To Diognetus*, 1.1.

64. *To Diognetus*, 10.4.

also be manifest in Diognetus's showing to others that very patience or long suffering that God had already shown to Diognetus and to all humanity. That patience, born of God's goodness, had been markedly shown by God in the "timing" of the incarnation;[65] and it would further be evidenced in God's having, as it were, mercifully "delayed" the final sentencing of humanity in order that humanity "which, in the past, had by [its] own actions been proved unworthy of life, might now be deemed worthy."[66] That patience—required of Diognetus in imitation of God's ongoing goodness—was, however, required not just of Diognetus but of *all* and *any* who would become lovers of God and so imitators of his goodness. Hence, it was required of, as indeed it was shown by, both the *writer* of the *Letter to Diognetus,* as he sought to explain and to commend the faith that Diognetus was investigating, and *Christians*, as and when, for example, they were persecuted. So, acting with a godly patience, the letter writer did not condone any ignorance or wrongdoing on Diognetus's part, even as God had not condoned the ignorance and the wickedness wrought by humanity prior to the Son's first coming.

Yet, while not condoning any ignorance or wrongdoing, the letter-writer did not then immediately condemn any such ignorance or wrongdoing on Diognetus's part, even as God had not immediately condemned sinful humanity. Rather, the letter writer sought to give Diognetus the information and the time that would permit an unforced appropriation of the truth of Christianity and the ensuing amendment of life, even as God did to humanity. So, where Diognetus was ignorant concerning certain aspects of Christian belief and practice, the letter writer patiently sought to *inform* him. Where Diognetus was in

65. *To Diognetus,* 8.7—9.2.
66. *To Diognetus,* 9.1.

the wrong, he patiently sought to *correct* him. Where Diognetus was uncommitted to the truth, to the one true God, he patiently sought to *encourage commitment*. Yet, for all such patience, even as God, who willed the salvation of all by persuasion and not by compulsion, had warned humanity that God's patience was not endless, the letter writer also warned Diognetus that "the real death kept for those who are condemned to the eternal fire"[67] would, in the absence of Diognetus's mending his ways, indeed eventually be exacted of Diognetus.

That same sense of a final sentencing, but patiently delayed that in the meanwhile sinful humanity might accept God's gift of "his own Son as a ransom for all"[68] and so not suffer that final sentencing of "punishment to the end,"[69] also appears in the writings of other mid-to-late second-century Apologists. It surfaces, for example, when they commended Christians who, when persecuted, did not curse but blessed their persecutors, thereby patiently creating an opportunity for their persecutors to discern God's mercy, to amend their lives, and so find themselves now not condemned to the eternal fires of the final judgement.

That seemingly gentler message, here seemingly whispered, was, however, often drowned out by the louder and more persistent proclamation of the sentence to come. Such seems to be the case in the writing of an Apologist like Tatian. Tatian aside, the *Letter to Diognetus* perhaps made more audible that which was whispered elsewhere and so promoted more obviously the love of God, rather than the fear of punishment, as a motive higher in order of praiseworthiness for commending a person's turning to God. Indeed, the *Letter to Diognetus* perhaps more clearly highlights the Apologists's

67. *To Diognetus*, 10.7.
68. *To Diognetus*, 9.2.
69. *To Diognetus*, 10.7.

understanding, shared with those for whom they wrote, not only *that* they should be involved in God's mission but also *how* they should be involved.

In retrospect, it is clear that the arguments of the Apologists were not just theoretical, theological arguments, voiced in the court of public debate and marshalled in defense of Christian beliefs and practices. They were theological, but not theoretical arguments, framed, at one and the same time, both to explain and defend Christianity and to commend to everyone the living of that particular faith, even *in extremis*.

Indeed, in so commending the Christian faith, the Apologists democratized the religious life. For, whereas in wider society a life of continence was commonly held to be the preserve of the philosopher, in the church the vocation to a life of sanctity was thought to be that of *everyone*, men and women, young and old. Witness Justin's record of the lives of an older woman and a younger man. The former had once lived a drunken life, often behaving immorally, not only with her immoral husband, but even with their servants and hirelings. In time she became a Christian. Initially she was minded to divorce her still immoral husband. However, this she did not do. For she had being persuaded that perhaps her new way of life might prompt her husband to amend his ways. Sadly, his ways only turned yet further for the worse. So, eventually she served him with a bill of divorce, a *repudium*, "that she might not, by continuing in her marriage to him and by sharing his board and his bed, become a partaker also in his wickedness and impiety."[70] The younger man, of whom Justin also wrote, was fervently opposed to any form of living a life of promiscuous intercourse. He therefore petitioned Felix, the governor of Alexandria, that he might be castrated. His petition—not

70. Justin, *Apology*, 2.2.

surprisingly given the then imperials policies of Domitian, Hadrian, and Antoninus Pius[71]—was flatly refused. Not downcast, the youth therefore decided to remain single, "satisfied with both his own approving conscience and the approval of those who thought as he did," a way of life, as Justin noted, markedly in contrast with that of the young Antinous.[72] Put another way, the two lives mentioned above, like the arguments composed in response to the charges brought against Christians of involvement in Thyestean feasts and Oedipean intercourse, served not just as examples of how Christians in fact lived, but also as challenges, or maybe invitations, to any who would accept them, to live as Christians in fact lived. For these challenges were framed in an encouraging way—if an ordinary wife, in a moral mess, in a very immoral household could break loose of sin and evil, and if a young, red-blooded youth could live a chaste life, so could any other person, whatever their past, their education, and their social status. In short, the God of the Christians sought the sanctification of, not the few, but the whole *demos*.

QUESTIONS FOR REFLECTION AND DISCUSSION

1. What should it mean for a twenty-first century Christian to be "in the world what the soul is in the body"?

2. According to the Apologists, God eventually condemned unrepentant sinners. However, according to a number of the same Apologists, prior to that final judgement, and in order that sinners might be given more time in which to repent, the same God showed

71. See Suetonius, *Domitian*, 7.1; Ulpian in *Digests* 48.8.4.2; Modestinus, in *Digests* 68.8.8.11.

72. Justin, *Apology*, 1.29.

patient forbearance. How should Christians balance patience, forbearance, judgement, and condemnation when relating to those who have sinned against them?

3. For moral reasons Tatian and Theophilos refused both to view certain statues and to attend particular plays. What should be the role of morality when deciding which art galleries should be visited, which plays attended, which films, television shows, and the like watched?

4. What, if anything, should the early Christian practice of rescuing exposed infants who had been left by parents to die say about how children should be valued and treated by contemporary societies?

5. The ethical teaching of the early Apologists on such issues as virginity, sex within marriage, remarriage, and same-sex relationships nowadays may seem quaint. What, if anything, may we learn from these second-century Christians regarding sexual ethics?

POSTSCRIPT

BECAUSE OF THE VERY nature of letters, their writers give later readers, not a complete insight into, but a selective appreciation of certain aspects of their thinking. This is, generally speaking, also the case when it comes to the mid-to-late second-century Apologists. For their writings are essentially those of letter writers, sometimes extended theological and philosophical letters, formally addressed to the emperor, but letters nevertheless. While therefore it is difficult sometimes to discern from these letters the Apologists's wider theological themes, it is not impossible. One theme, in particular, that of *creation*, may be found there. For while the charges of atheism, cannibalism, and incest were significant charges, demanding proper responses, in certain ways, theologically speaking, these charges were but presenting issues. For behind them lay questions concerning the proper appreciation both of creation, understood not simply as that in contradistinction with humanity, but as all that has been created, humanity included, and of the holy ways in which the whole of creation should relate to itself and to its Maker. For central to the defense against the charge of atheism lay the thought that *creation*—whether in the form of the celestial bodies studied by the astrologists, or the "gods" of the Hellenistic poems and plays, or the statues of the Greco-Roman cults, or the emperors—*was not to be worshipped*. For each and all of these had been made, and so were on the "made" side of the "made/Maker" distinction.

Axiomatic to refuting the charge of cannibalism, which, like the Hellenistic practices of exposing unwanted infants to the elements and of staging gladiatorial shows, involved killing a fellow human being, was the belief that *creation was not to be abused*. For human beings had been brought into being in order to live and flourish, and not to be hurried, especially by fellow human beings, to death.

Underlying the response to the charges by non-Christians of Christian involvement in incestuous and adulterous behavior, and, by extension, behind the Apologists's critique of males seeking improper delight in the female form, even if only as encountered in and through statues of the female form, was the wish to urge that *creation's pure and proper interrelatedness should not to be sullied*, let alone sacrificed on the altar of sexual self-gratification.

Behind the various replies to these three charges was an understanding of creation as both good, to be honored but not worshipped, and as reflecting in its intra-relationships, creature to creature, its Creator's gracious, faithful, and just relationship to all creation. In short, the defenses marshalled by the Apologists against these three anti-Christian charges were undergirded, to a large extent, by the theological imperative to *appreciate creation as that made*, essentially distinct but not divided from its Maker, and to *treat it well*.

Certainly there are aspects of the Apologists's arguments that may seem to detract or even do detract from the assertion that matter, made by God, is good and so is to be treated well. The writer of the *Letter to Diognetus*, for example, refers to Christians as those who "live in their own countries, but only as strangers."[1] This might be taken to suggest that "their own countries" are to be avoided, or, at least, held at arm's length. But appearances may here be deceptive. Those Christians are not to be thought of as being homeless strangers in this world. Rather, they are to be understood as being the "strangers and pilgrims on the earth" of Hebrews 11:13. They are those who, while living "in the flesh" do not live "according to the flesh," but "walk . . . after the Spirit."[2] So, for example, they are "strangers" to the practice of casting out any unwanted children. While they share their table generously with all, they are entire strangers to sharing their marriage bed with any but their spouses. The Christians referred to here, rather than belying creation's goodness, are therefore those who sought to confirm it as its Maker intended it to be.

By contrast, perhaps the prioritizing by certain Apologists of living a virginal life over a married life, and certainly the critique of a second marriage as gilded adultery, do undermine, to varying degrees, the assertion that creation is good. Yet, in comparison with gnostic Christians, for whom both matter was the result of either an accident or the malevolence of a heavenly, powerful Demiurge and the world was but a prison to be escaped, the Apologists generally affirmed creation, whether enjoyed by a virgin or a married individual, as good.

What then was held, generally speaking, to be true of the whole creation was also held to be true of the many

1. *To Diognetus*, 5.5.
2. Romans 8:4. See also 2 Corinthians 10:2–3.

parts of creation. So, for example, individuals, even the poor and the unimportant person, mattered. Acts of charity and not just words, even if these words were kind words, were required. Although not drawing explicitly upon the thinking of the Letter of James, with its castigating anyone who greets the ill-clad and the hungry, saying, Go in peace, and be warm and filled, but without giving them any food or clothing,[3] the majority of the Apologists stressed that acts of charity that addressed the very particular material needs of their fellow creatures were significant. Individual histories, written in the contingent, creaturely world, were to be cherished. So, again as an example, Christ's words on the cross, "forgive them, for they know not what they are doing," were to be inhabited by Christians, and were, through Christians similarly accepting the anger of others, yet without hostility, both to evidence all people's common but fragile creatureliness and to foster relationships befitting creation's natural kinship. For gnostic Christians, a person's history was "transcendent," each life being but a cipher of those of all others, with no-one's particular "immanent" history being of any significance. In marked contrast, for the Apologists, history concerned individually lived lives, broken, forgiven, and healed, reshaped and brought to maturity in response to the God who ultimately would be the judge of each and all.

Whilst for the Apologists generally the world was good, it was, however, good in a derivative, or secondary sense of the word "good." Two examples will suffice to evidence this. An emperor, for the Apologists, was not the source, as some Greco-Roman thinkers maintained, of the empire's peace and justice, and so was not to be treated as such. Rather, he was God's appointed agent, called to administer God's justice and to establish God's peace, in the

3. James 2:15–16.

empire as in heaven. It was in this secondary sense that the emperor might be called "good." Equally, the world's order was deemed to be good, but again in a secondary sense. For it properly was not the absolute source whereby a person might be led to know God, but one of God's means by which a person might be graciously helped to discern the harmonious Maker and Mover of all.

That the material world—and again it must be emphasized that humans are included under the general headings of "the world," "the material world," and the like—was held by the Apologists to be good and so to be valued is even suggested by their shared warnings that eventually, in and through the final judgement, all shall be faced with divine judgement. For, as the warnings, implied both in the judgements made through the Hebrew prophets and through the holy lives of second-century Christians, were given in order to prompt the transformation of those then living unworthily, so the purpose of both the repeated warnings and the descriptions of the final judgement was to be creative. For God was held to speak creatively, directing people to acknowledge their own God-given worth and to live accordingly, honoring their neighbor as their God-given self, and worshipping the only God, the Bestower upon all creatures of their glorious worth. Certainly warnings of a future, final judgement did emphasize that God took seriously sinful acts that, as well as dishonoring the Holy One, also devalued and marred the sinner and those sinned against. However, in addition to emphasizing sin's seriousness, these warnings also pointed to God's readiness to grant sinners, before it was too late, an opportunity to repent, amend their lives, and accept being recreated as new creatures. So, the repeated warnings of the Apologists concerning the final judgement paradoxically emphasized their sense of God's valuing creation, that of which the Maker and Mover of all clearly was loathed to wash his hands.

This generally shared emphasis on the goodness of the world in all its various parts, the Apologists then applied in a form of theological materialism. So, because the so-called gods of the empire's cults and theaters were creatures made by creaturely sculptors and dramatists, they were not to be worshipped. Because the emperor and, by extension, the empire with all its powers were creatures, they were not to be worshipped. Prayers were not to be made to the emperor. General sacrifices demanded by the imperial powers were not to be offered. Neither the emperor nor the empire were to be understood as the origin of all that was good. God alone was such. Neither were they to be treated as absolute authorities, having the "final say" everywhere and always. For the Creator was the Lord of all lords, from whom alone came "all good counsels."[4]

For the same reason the emperor and, by extension, the empire were to be accountable servants of the Maker of all, God's instrument for the well-being of all. The emperor therefore was to be a vehicle of God's justice and peace for each and every person, whatever an individual's status or condition. The empire, meanwhile, was always to be mindful of the One by and through whom all governing authorities had been instituted,[5] and so open to, amongst other matters, heeding principled religious dissent. So, for example, the empire was to honor the religious freedom of the mid-to-late second-century Christians not to participate in the imperial cult. Honor, however, was to be paid to the emperor where honor was due. So, as and when the emperor enabled peace and exercised just laws—and by "peace" and "just laws" were meant "the peace of God" and

4. *Book of Common Prayer*. Second Collect at Evening Prayer.

5. Romans 13:1.

"the laws of God"—fellow creatures, Christians included, were to pray to God *for* the emperor and to work with the emperor and his officials in the promotion of God's peace and justice for all.

What was true of the emperor was also true of all other humans, no matter how high their status. For, since they also were creatures and since no creatures should be worshipped, no humans might be worshipped. Not even an emperor's favorite, an Antinous, was to be worshipped. Not even an emperor's favorite who had lived a laudable and innocent life—something that an Antinous could not claim—was to be worshipped. For the grounds for being worshipped lay, not in being a creature, however exalted, nor in deeds, however noble and good, but in being God.

Further, what was true of the emperor in his role as one with responsibilities for the well-being of others was also true of all humans, however high or lowly their status. For, as creatures, who shared a common creature-liness, every person was to be concerned for their fellow creatures. So, they were to be hospitable one to another, but only insofar as that hospitality was consistent with the inter-relatedness that God ordered, as is evidenced in the assertion that hospitality was not to extend to the marriage bed. All offspring, being gifts from God, were to be cherished. Not one single child was to be exposed. Spouses were to be faithful, the one to the other. In permitting divorce, albeit in a very particular circumstance, Justin may initially seem to have undermined, at least partially, the theological materialism expressed in and through matrimonial vows. Certainly Justin wrote approvingly of a wife who, on becoming a Christian, eventually divorced her increasingly intemperate and dissolute husband.[6] Yet, in reality, such a divorce in such a particular situation may amount, less to

6. Justin, *Apology*, 2.2.

an undermining of theological materialism and more to a sustaining matter's value in difficult circumstances. For initially this wife stayed in her marital relationship, in the hope that her husband might realize afresh his God-given worth and appreciate anew the worth of his marriage, the honest reciprocal love that was the fulfilling of God's law;[7] and eventually, in divorced him, she chose the lesser of two evils, in part so as to protect her own God-given value. Pastoral theology here may be qualifying doctrine. Yet it may be doing so, both out of a recognition of human failure and through the wish to honor not only the matter that was constituted by the once married, now divorced woman, but also her particular history shaped in the materiality of an individual's contingent life.

Interestingly, this concern for one's fellow creatures the Apologists did not limit to a Christian's concern for another Christian. They acknowledged that often it did center on a Christian's love for another Christian; but they also recognized that properly it also extended to a love for all others. So Christians, and by extension all godly people, were to show concern, for example, for the poor and homeless, the hungry man so in want that, in order that he might eat, he was ready to sell himself to be a competitor in a gladiatorial show, even though he had not the slightest chance of surviving. Likewise all were to safeguard the young and innocent, lest they might be morally corrupted by the lewd *dramatis personae* of the plays to which their parents unwisely might bring them.

Such an emphasis upon creatureliness ensured that the writings of the Apologists were not exclusively anthropocentric, with humans being portrayed as a creaturely élite. So the Apologists were content to write of creation's role in facilitating humans to know the Maker and Mover of all. The Apologists's treatments of, for example, the stars evidenced

7. See Romans 13:8.

this. The creatureliness of the stars asked humans not to worship them, nor to view them as that which astrologists should consult in order to attempt to discern a person's destiny; and the movement of the stars invited people to look beyond them to the One who moved them. So, in and through their moved creatureliness, the stars, like all other creatures, sought, to paraphrase the apostle Paul, to warn people against exchanging the truth of God for a lie by worshipping the creature rather than the Creator.[8]

Nor was such pointing humans to the Mover of all things something that was time-limited, an activity that humans might ultimately disregard. For the Apologists held that the goal of the religious quest differed from that envisaged, for example, by a Philo. The former viewed moved matter as constantly pointing a person, no matter how spiritually mature, to the Mover of all. The latter, on the other hand, understood the religious quest as involving the soul's gradual detachment from the material and external and transient to the spiritual and the interior and the eternal, that, by grace, the vision of the simple God might be realized.[9] Certainly the Apologists did think that people should, in some sense, distance or detach themselves from the moved world of matter, in order to be rendered ever more "apt" for the vision of God. Yet, alongside this recommending that people distance themselves or detach themselves from the moved world of matter, the Apologists also advocated that the same people should attach themselves to the selfsame world. For this distancing was to be undertaken in order that the world of matter might not be treated as an end in itself, an "idolized god," whilst the attachment was to be such that people might be led, through the movement of all that has been made, to discern God, the Maker

8. Romans 1:25.

9. See Philo, *On Abraham*, 195–6; Philo, *On Dreams*, 1.60.

and Mover of all. Any detachment was lest people might be "trapped" by the world that they were contemplating, and so be diverted from honoring the Maker of the world to honoring only that made; and all attachment was that the very same people, attending to the world as an instrument by which God chose to reveal himself, might continuously be drawn to contemplating the world's Mover and theirs. For a Philo and a number of the Apologists there was then this need to attend to the world of matter as a sign, but to attend to it in such a way as not to exclude the attending to the One to whom the sign pointed. When, however, it came to any distancing, any distancing, for one such as Philo, led, in the end, to a compete stepping away, a relinquishing the complex world of matter for the single, simple God. In contrast, for the Apologists, any withdrawing was the stepping away from that made, lest, being captivated by creation, one might exchange the worship of the Creator for that of the created. For the one therefore matter would ultimately prove to be a hindrance, while for the other it was to be ever a help, a consequence of it being the good creation of the good Creator.

Suggestions, especially in the context of heated arguments, that the imperial cult involved the worship of dumb, blind statues and that Christians engaged in atheism, cannibalism, and incest could, all too readily, descend into something akin to the cries of an audience at a modern day pantomime, with Christians saying to non-Christians, "your statues are idols," only to elicit the reply, "Oh, no, they're not," and with non-Christians arguing, "You Christians are cannibals," with Christians answering, "Oh, no, we're not." The undergirding therefore by the Apologists of their arguments with a doctrine of creation, even if generally that doctrine maintained the making of all from pre-existent, unformed matter, *hulē*, rather than "from nothing," the latter of which doctrines appears to have emerged only slowly and uncertainly,[10] certainly opened the possibility of lifting reactions by pagans to charges by the Christians, and *vice versa*, above the superficial. Further, it permitted a more thinking citizen, who might not accept as authoritative the scriptural texts severally marshalled by the Apologists, to recall the widely acknowledged idea that behind the moved world there lay an Unmover Mover, a notion not wholly inconsistent with the belief that behind all that was made was the Creator God. In short, it would seem that the Apologists's undergirding their Apologies with a doctrine of creation lent gravitas to arguments that otherwise might have seemed a little pejorative, and so might have been dismissed all too readily, without a thought, and to no one's edification.

10. See Louth, *The origins of the Christian Mystical Tradition*, 75. See also Stead, *The Platonism of Arius*, 25–31; Grant, *Miracle and Natural Law*, 133–152.

Appendix

GENERAL HISTORY OUTLINE

General history	Christian history	Literature
10BC–AD40 Philo *floruit*		
c.37 Josephus is born		
54–68 Nero, Emperor		
64 Great fire in Rome	64 Neronian persecutions	
69–79 Vespasian, Emperor Policy of Romanization and urbanization in the Roman provinces is advanced		

General history	Christian history	Literature
79–81 Titus, Emperor		
81–96 Domitian, Emperor 96 Domitian murdered The cult of the emperor is developed	96 Domitian's persecution of Christians, in Rome and then in the Roman province of Asia	
96–98 Nerva, Emperor	Some relaxation of measures against both Christians and Jews	
98–117 Trajan, Emperor		
100 Josephus died		
101–102 War against the Dacians		
105–106 Further warring against the Dacians		
112–113 Pliny's mission in Bithynia with Pontus	112–113 Pliny corresponds with the emperor Trajan	
114–117 Roman war against Parthia		115 Tacitus wrote of the Neronian persecutions
117–138 Hadrian, Emperor		120 Suetonius wrote of the Neronian persecutions

General history	Christian history	Literature
	124 Hadrian's Rescript to Minucius Fundanus, proconsul of Asia, concerning Christians	
130 Antinous died	c.130 Justin becomes a Christian	
138–161 Antoninus Pius, Emperor		c.145. Aelius Aristides, *Panegyric to Rome*
		c.145 Aristides, *Apology*
		c.150 *The Letter to Diognetus*
	154–155 Polycarp in Rome	c.155. Justin Martyr, *Apology* I
	156 Polycarp martyred in Smyrna	
	c.160 Marcion died	c.160. Justin Martyr, *Dialogue with Trypho*
		c.155–165. Tatian, *Address to the Greeks*
161 Commodus born		161. Justin Martyr, *Apology* II
161–180 Marcus Aurelius, Emperor		

General history	Christian history	Literature
165 Plague spreads from Mesopotamia to the eastern provinces of the Roman empire, then to Rome and the Rhineland	165 Justin martyred in Rome	
167–180 Germanic tribes exert pressure on the Roman frontiers on the Danube	165–170, 175–177 Sporadic persecutions of Christians in the Roman province of Asia	
	c.170 Theophilos elected bishop of Antioch	
	177 Pogroms at Lyons and Vienne. Vettius Epagathus and Attalus martyred	176–178 Athenagoras, *Plea*
	178 Irenaeus elected bishop of Lyons	c.170 Celsus, *True Reason*
180–192 Commodus, Marcus Aurelius' son, Emperor	180 Scillitan martyrs, Carthage	180 Theophilos, *Letter to Autolycus*
c.185 Marcia, mistress of Commodus, becomes a Christian	Catechetical school at Alexandria founded by Pantaenus [died c.190]	180–200 Clement of Alexandria *floruit*
	185 Origen born	c.185 Irenaeus, *Against the heresies*

BIBLIOGRAPHY

PRIMARY SOURCES

The Acts of Justin and his Companions. In *The Acts of the Christian Martyrs*, texts and translations by Herbert Musurillo, 42–61. Oxford Early Christian Texts. Oxford: Oxford University Press, 1972. For another English translation, see *A New Eusebius: Documents Illustrating the History of the Church to AD 337*, edited by J. Stephenson, revised with additional documents by W. H. C. Frend, 32–34. London: SPCK, 1987.

Aelius Aristides. *Oration XXVI: Panegyric to Rome.* In *Aelius Aristides, Orations.* Vol. 2, edited by B. Keil, 91–124. Berlin: Weidmann, 1898.

The Apostolic Fathers. Edited and translated by Bart D. Ehrman. Loeb Classical Library, Vol. 2. Cambridge: Harvard University Press, 2003.

Aristides. *Apology.* In *The Apology of Aristides on behalf of the Christians,* from a Syriac MS. preserved on Mount Sinai. Edited with an introduction and translation by J. Rendel Harris, with an appendix containing the main portion of the original Greek text by J. Armitage Robinson. Texts and Studies, Vol. 1.1. Cambridge: Cambridge University Press, 1891.

Athenagoras. *Plea.* In Athenagoras, *Legatio* and *De Resurrectione*, edited and translated by William R. Schoedel, 2–87. Oxford Early Christian Texts. Oxford: Oxford University Press, 1972.

Bibliography

Basilides. See Eusebius, *Ecclesiastical History* 4.7.7.

Dio Cassius. *Epitome*. In *A New Eusebius. Documents Illustrating the History of the Church to AD 337*, edited by J. Stephenson; revised with additional documents by W. H. C. Frend, 6. London: SPCK, 1987.

To Diognetus. In *Early Christian Fathers*, translated and edited by Cyril C. Richardson, in collaboration with Eugene R. Fairweather, Edward Rochie Hardy and Massey Hamilton Shepherd, 213–24. The Library of Christian Classics, Vol. 1. London: SCM, 1953.

To Diognetus. In *The Epistle to Diognetus: The Greek Text with Introduction, Translation and Notes* by H. C. Meecham. Manchester: Manchester University Press, 1949.

Eusebius. *Ecclesiastical History*. In *The History of the Church*. Translated by G. A. Williamson; revised and edited with a new introduction by Andrew Louth. London: Penguin, 1989.

Irenaeus. *Against the Heretics*. In *The Ante-Nicene Fathers*, Vol. 1. Edited by Alexander Roberts and James Donald. Reprint, Grand Rapids: Eerdmans, 1981.

John Chrysostom. *Against the Jews*. In *Patrologia Graeca*, Vol. 48, 843–944. Paris: Migne, 1862.

Justin. *Apology 1 & 2*, and *Dialogue with Trypho*. In *The Ante-Nicene Fathers*, Vol. 1. Edited by Alexander Roberts and James Donald. Reprint, Grand Rapids: Eerdmans, 1981.

The Letter of the Churches of Lyons and Vienne. In *The Acts of the Christian Martyrs*, texts and translations by Herbert Musurillo, 62–85. Oxford Early Christian Texts. Oxford: Oxford University Press, 1972.

The Martyrdom of Perpetua and Felicitas. In *The Acts of the Christian Martyrs*, texts and translations by Herbert Musurillo, 106–31. Oxford Early Christian Texts. Oxford: Oxford University Press, 1972.

The Martyrdom of Polycarp. In *The Acts of the Christian Martyrs*, texts and translations by Herbert Musurillo, 2–21. Oxford Early Christian Texts. Oxford: Oxford University Press, 1972.

Origen. *Against Celsus*. In *Contra Celsum*. Translated by Henry Chadwick. Cambridge: Cambridge University Press, 1953.

Philo. *On Dreams*. Edited and translated by F. H. Coulson and G. H. Whitaker, 294–579. Loeb Classical Library, Vol. 5. Cambridge: Harvard University Press, 1934.

Bibliography

————. *On Flight and Finding*. Edited and translated by F. H. Coulson and G. H. Whitaker, 10–125. Loeb Classical Library, Vol. 5. Cambridge: Harvard University Press, 1934.

————. *On the Migration of Abraham*. Edited and translated by F. H. Coulson and G. H. Whitaker, 132–267. Loeb Classical Library, Vol. 4. Revised and reprinted, Cambridge: Harvard University Press, 1939.

Pliny. *The Letters of Pliny: A History and Social Commentary*. Edited by A. N. Sherwin-White. Oxford: Oxford University Press, 1966.

————. *Fifty Letters of Pliny*. Selected and edited with introduction and notes by A. N. Sherwin-White. 2nd ed. Oxford: Oxford University Press 1969. English translations of the letters to which I refer may be found in *A New Eusebius: Documents Illustrating the History of the Church to AD 337*, edited by J. Stephenson, revised with additional documents by W. H. C. Frend, 18–21. London: SPCK, 1987.

The Sibylline Oracles 3. In *Book III of The Sibylline Oracles and Its Social Setting*. With an introduction, translation, and commentary by Rieuwerd Buitenwerf. Studia in Veteris Testamenti Pseudepigrapha, Vol. 17. Leiden: Brill, 2003.

Tatian. *Address*. In Tatian, *Oratio ad Graecos* and Fragments. Edited and translated by Molly Whittaker. Oxford Early Christian Texts. Oxford: Oxford University Press, 1982.

Tertullian. *Apology*. In *The Ante-Nicene Fathers*, Vol. 3. Edited by Alexander Roberts and James Donaldson. Reprint, Grand Rapids: Eerdmans, 1980.

Theophilos. *To Autolycus*. In *Theophilos ad Autolycum*. Text and translation by Robert M. Grant. Oxford Early Christian Texts. Oxford: Oxford University Press, 1970.

SECONDARY SOURCES

Grant, Robert M. *The Greek Apologists of the Second Century*. London: SCM, 1988.

————. *Miracle and Natural Law in Graeco-Roman and Early Christian Thought*. 1952. Reprint, Eugene, OR: Wipf & Stock, 2011.

Grillmeier, Aloys, SJ. *Christ in Christian Tradition, Vol. 1, From the Apostolic Age to Chalcedon 451*. 2nd rev. ed. London: Mowbrays, 1975.

Bibliography

Head, P. M. "Tatian's Christology and Its Influence in the Composition of the Diatessaron." *Tyndale Bulletin* 43 (1992) 121–37.

Holmes, Michael W. *The Apostolic Fathers*. Grand Rapids: Baker, 1989.

Hurtado, Larry. *Destroyer of the Gods: Early Christian Distinctiveness in the Roman World*. Baylor, TX: Baylor University Press, 2016.

Jefford, C. N. *The Epistle to Diognetus (with the Fragments of Quadratus)*. Oxford: Oxford University Press, 2013.

Kelly, J. N. D. *Early Christian Doctrine*. 4th ed. London: A & C Black, 1968.

Louth, Andrew. *The Origins of the Christian Mystical Tradition: From Plato to Denys*. Oxford: Clarendon, 1981.

Osborn, Eric. *The Emergence of Christian Theology*. Cambridge: Cambridge University Press, 1993.

Pedersen, W. L. "Tatian the Assyrian." In *Companion to Second Century Christian "Heretics,"* edited by A. Marjanen and P. Luomanen, 125–58. Vigiliae Christianae, Supp. 76. Leiden: Brill, 2005.

Rhee, Helen. *Early Christian Literature: Christ and Culture in the Second and Third Centuries*. Early Church Monographs. Abingdon, UK: Routledge, 2005.

Stark, Rodney. *The Rise of Christianity: A Sociologist Reconsiders History*. Princeton, NJ: Princeton University Press, 1996.

Stead, G. C. "The Platonism of Arius." *The Journal of Theological Studies* n.s. 15 (1964) 14–31.

SUBJECT INDEX

ANCIENT DOCUMENT INDEX